The natural
Bliss of Being

The Natural Bliss of Being

By Jackson Peterson

Dedication

This book is dedicated to my daughter Kia.
Although her life was all too brief, through her gentle
and completely open heart, she led me to discover that *the natural
bliss of being* is a treasure that we all share within ourselves.

Acknowledgment

Tashi Mannox: Tibetan Style Script Title Design
Connor Fitzgerald: Illustrator and Cover Design

I would like to thank my wife, Matthia, for her editorial comments
and spiritual support.

I also would like to thank my children: Rishi, Jack,and Nikki, for
their spiritual and emotional support as well as for their suggestions
regarding the book. And thanks to my two grandchildren,
Lily and Mia, who inspired me to keep the book simple enough
that anyone should be able to find the book an "easy read."

Table of Contents

Introduction

I believe deeply that we must find, all of us together, a new spirituality. This new concept ought to be elaborated alongside the religions in such a way that all people of good will could adhere to it.
H.H. Tenzin Gyatso,
The 14th Dalai Lama

Today there appears to be a strong interest in learning more about who we are, what we are, and how to maximize our sense of well-being. For many the pace and shallowness of our daily work and life routines often lead to a sense of dissatisfaction with ourselves and our sense of purpose in life. Much of this can be attributed to social conditions and the economic demands placed on us. We seem to be working more yet we are enjoying our lives less. Stress is certainly one aspect of everyone's life, and it seems that in today's uncertain economic times a great deal of that stress revolves around job security, managing our financial obligations, affording higher education, and providing for our families. These appear to be causative factors regarding our angst and existential dissatisfaction, but the real causes lie within our thought processes and how we manage our lives and stress internally. External circumstances have no specific ability to determine how we react to them. Our ability to maintain some sense of happiness is directly dependent on how well we understand

and manage our inner life, the one aspect of our lives that we may be able to directly control if we have the correct means and know-how.

However, happiness doesn't occur in a vacuum. Happiness is a resulting quality of experience that is grounded in an overall sense of harmony and essential meaning within the context of one's overall life. Life is relationship. Life is connection. Life is exchange. Life is experience. The sense of deep satisfaction and contentment available is proportional to the depth of one's perceived engagement with life through experience on many different levels. For some it's being in love and having a family. But even then we tend to ponder beyond the surface aspects of our existence and yearn for a deeper insight into the mystery we call life. For some, a religious or spiritual connection can give this deeper sense of meaning and aesthetic symmetry in life. The feeling that there is some deeper significance to our lives as expressed and experienced through belief and faith in a spiritual dimension seems to have been part of mankind's psyche since earliest times. A spiritual connection or belief can also foster a sense of deeper purpose, a purpose that is aligned with some grand scheme or divine plan that makes sense ultimately of all of life's apparent chaos.

Literally all cultures had and continue to have some form of a spiritual or religious belief system in place. And within those religious or spiritual traditions there were those who either claimed or actually had developed deeper connections with the mysterious forces that govern and inhabit the spiritual world. In the most ancient cultures before the dawn of civilization, there were the shamans, the mediators between this world and the unseen worlds beyond. As civilization developed, the complexities of religious and spiritual life also developed creating an entire class of professional priests and their organized bureaucracy. However, there still were those few rare souls who had the unique capacity and proclivity to understand and experience the deepest levels of spiritual consciousness and realization. Generically speaking these spiritually gifted people were known as mystics and seers. Some were authentic and others were charlatans. But the authentic ones stood out as being truly unique in their personal presence as well as their teachings. World religions all began from one person sharing their experience and vision of a spiritual dimension that lies beyond our ordinary material world. Most not only left a message, but also left a path or way for others to follow.

There seems to have been two sets of teachings in most cases, the exoteric and the esoteric. The exoteric was for the masses who were just content to believe and follow the rules that would eventually lead to salvation or realization upon death. A much smaller group of adherents were interested in direct spiritual experience. These were the followers and practitioners of the esoteric path of mystical gnosis, enlightenment, and practice. All the major religious traditions had this type of division in place, not by design as much as by the natural inclinations of a populace. The followers of the esoteric or mystical schools were always in the minority and were a much more sensitive and intuitive group in general. They pondered the mysteries and meaning of life as opposed to being just good "worker bees" in the social structure. It is from this unique and spiritually gifted group that most of a culture's wealth of mystical poetry, prose, art, and teaching lineages arose. The legacy of spiritual teachings had a timeless quality that future generations would savor and treasure above all other products of social endeavor. These teachings and the art forms they engendered embodied the living soul of a culture as expressed in its literature, art, architecture, and religion.

It was initially as a teenager that I was attracted by the Zen-inspired art forms of Japan and China and also the mystical poetry of the Sufis, or Islamic mystics. When I was twelve, I fell in love with the eleventh-century *Rubaiyat of Omar Khayyam* and began to learn Persian in order to read the verses in their native language. All this eventually led to a further inquiry and pursuit of the innermost spiritual teachings that Eastern religions had to offer. I have spent more than forty-five years of my life, since the age of sixteen, exploring various pathways and methods that offer means for a person to discover their own inner treasury of well-being, happiness, and spiritual illumination. I studied Zen Buddhism in China, Japan, Korea, and the United States with various Zen masters. I studied and practiced Tibetan Buddhism, initially in Nepal and later with several masters or teachers of different traditions, especially Tibetan Dzogchen and Mahamudra. I studied and practiced Sufism in Kashmir, India, and Saudi Arabia with Sufi masters of several traditions. I studied and spent time in Israel learning the essential teachings of Kabbalah with Orthodox rabbis of the tradition. I studied and practiced the meditation methods within Orthodox or Eastern Christianity with Greek priests and an Egyptian Coptic priest in Jerusalem. I learned and practiced Taoist methods of inner energy work and Taoist yoga. I initially received teachings of meditation in India relating to methods called Kundalini yoga.

There were many other teachings that I explored and practiced, but those mentioned above had the greatest impact on my spiritual, psychological and emotional life. Because I had the good fortune of being exposed to so many authentic teachings and teachers, I was able to see and discern common themes and similar practices among the various traditions. I realized that the cultural context and languaging of those teachings often created a barrier for would-be students. There also appeared to be an ethnocentric bias inherent in almost all the traditions, which was a bit disturbing. Each tradition seemed to feel their tradition was uniquely superior to all others for various reasons embedded often within the cosmic or religious mythos of the tradition itself. I actually found this to be rather humorous, an impression I never shared.

But what I discovered in all cases was that there existed within these traditions a reservoir of great spiritual knowledge, wisdom, and enlightenment. My intention is to share some of my insights and offer practical methods that I have learned over these many years of research, study, and practice within these various traditions and on my own. I have developed an approach that is completely generic, nonreligious, and culturally neutral.

What I teach is not commonly available to most seekers. This is due to the fact that the traditions' most advanced teachings are typically reserved for "insiders" who have met all the prerequisite steps and "initiations." But unfortunately, those same advanced teachings often are the most powerful and most effective methods taught in the entire tradition. Many of the true wisdom-holders alive today are part of a generation of teachers that is disappearing from the planet. They came from a time when real effort and practice were expended in a way that today's modern life rarely allows. From their depth of practice came a depth of profound realization. And as part of that realization was the awareness that many of the most powerful, transformative, and enlightening teachings that had traditionally been considered secret and reserved for only a few highly qualified adepts needed to be taught more openly and become available broadly and for all students. Otherwise, they felt that the highest teachings, the actual crown jewels of the tradition's wisdom lineage, would die out forever. So to my great fortune, most of the masters I met with were willing to share the "crown jewels" of their highest and most revered teachings along with the instructions for implementation and practice. Many younger and more conservative teachers and students of the same traditions were shocked to learn what their teachers had taught me. I share all of these methods openly and present them in a completely generic manner.

I have found that within these teachings there is a body of knowledge that can be isolated and presented in a completely neutral language that is more similar to a branch of science like physics or biology. The religious traditions were simply a vehicle for a much more universal teaching regarding the nature of man in relationship to a spiritual world and origin. Aldous Huxley referred to this universal teaching as the *Perennial Philosophy*.

The introduction to his book *The Perennial Philosophy* begins:

> Rudiments of the Perennial Philosophy may be found among the traditionary lore of primitive peoples in every region of the world, and in its fully developed forms it has a place in every one of the higher religions. A version of this Highest Common Factor in all preceding and subsequent theologies was first committed to writing more than twenty-five centuries ago, and since that time the inexhaustible theme has been treated again and again, from the standpoint of every religious tradition and in all the principal languages of Asia and Europe.

For many years people have always asked me if I could recommend a good book that was not too bogged down in specific cultural or traditional teachings but was able to describe and prescribe a methodology of self-realization or enlightenment that anyone could read, understand, and apply. I usually suggested starting with Eckhart Tolle's excellent book *The Power of Now*. But then I also wanted to go much further and share the great wealth of insights and methodologies from the Eastern philosophies in a completely generic manner. So finally I decided to write *that* book myself. The first step was to translate the material culturally and present it in a completely generic manner.

Stripping off the cultural and denominational clothing as well as the ornamentation of these traditions reveals a body of incredible beauty, simplicity, directness, and applicability by anyone from any culture. Again, this is not unlike engaging in a study of a branch of science that requires no prior exposure to religious or cultural mythologies as a prerequisite. This is not to say that I am against the traditional lineage approaches to a spiritually transformative study and practice. There is a wonderful context of rich symbolism that ritual, liturgy, and religious belief can bring to one's experience. I am only saying that it is not necessary in order to glean the essential aspects of a spiritually transformative practice. And as seekers become more adept in their chosen wisdom tradition, the rituals and liturgies become less and less the focus anyway. But this is good for other reasons too. With our stripped-down model, it's much easier to find parallels among related traditions, but it is also easier to compare our model with a more secular and scientific point of view.

Instead of dealing with "evil demons" for instance, we are dealing with troublesome emotional states, fixed ideas, and a lack of cognitive clarity. We also can find ourselves able to converse within the world of psychotherapy and various models of mind/brain science more easily. As far as that goes, I also took neuroscience, brain and consciousness research, psychotherapy, and especially quantum physics to be my teachers as well. They taught me to look deeply into the processes and patterns involved in human experience in an effort to see a completely integrative and holistic world view. I see no conflict whatsoever between science and spiritual knowledge and practice. I see them rather to be quite compatible and mutually enlightening. The Dalai Lama is very supportive and participative in various neuroscience conferences regarding the brain and consciousness. He feels science can be very beneficial in uncovering the inner workings of the mind and how the brain relates to consciousness and awareness.

I wrote in the book:

> Another aspect of understanding who and what we are in the universe is offered today in cutting-edge scientific research and its spin-offs. I have been particularly interested in the philosophical and spiritual implications of quantum physics. Many quantum physicists since the 1930's have taken the position that consciousness or awareness itself is not a product of the brain, but may indeed

be part of the fabric of the universe itself at its most basic level, from the very beginning. I have spent many years studying this topic and have been very curious regarding the close linkages between Eastern thought and quantum physics. From these studies I am convinced that there is a Quantum Intelligence that pervades and informs all phenomena, on every level whether sub-atomic or on the macro-level. It is also from understanding the quantum aspects of consciousness regarding extra-sensory perception, such as telepathy and clairvoyance, that a more clear and scientific understanding of these phenomena is possible. I believe that it is this generic Quantum Intelligence that mystics and others have been tapping into for millennia and then describing according to their own cultural and religious milieu.

Some call this Quantum Intelligence, God or Allah, some Buddha Mind, or the Tao, others call it Self or Brahman. Whatever the name, I believe those names are pointing to the same Reality. And that Reality has an intimate relationship with our own states of mind and consciousness. It is not some external divine power that controls or observes us from without, but rather it is our own divinity that inspires us from within. One of the Desert Fathers of ancient Eastern Orthodox Christianity said, "To know your self is to know God."

We can discover a spiritual core of awareness within our consciousness that is intrinsically pure, changeless, unconditioned, and free. It is our own presence of awareness that exists in a default mode of perceiving. It can't be damaged or improved. Whether the body is alive or dead, it remains as the eye of experience. It's not something you possess, but rather it is who you actually are. It is this unchanging and timeless conscious awareness that is realized in moments of illumination and enlightenment. It is this primordially perfect consciousness that enlightened masters attempt to "point out" to their students. If successful, the students' perspective on life will suddenly be completely transformed forever. It is this realization to which all teachers and masters of the esoteric traditions are pointing. I call this ever-present consciousness Quantum Intelligence or Awareness, as it pervades all levels and aspects of reality.

What I teach and have been teaching for several years in retreats, group meditation classes, and private sessions are the most essential and advanced methods that facilitate this sudden self-revelation. This book will offer "pointing-out" instructions and approaches that anyone without prior experience should be able to use easily with great success. Typically most paths and teachers offer an approach that is based on a gradual process of transformation and purification. Much time is spent on fixing, improving, and modifying existing states of mind. One tries to improve the personality and self in a process of "becoming" enlightened. The approach I discuss is much more radical; it's based on recognizing that inner core of our consciousness that is *already* perfect and enlightened and requires no correction or improvement. It is unconditioned and "defect-free" since the beginning of time, but we don't notice it. Instead, our minds are constantly engaged in another level of consciousness that is centered around the mind's sense of "me," my story, and what's mine. And it is this *me* fixation that is the cause of 100 percent of our emotional suffering. It's as though we are walking around in a daydream most of the time, we are so absorbed in our personal stories. The methods I share have the ability to snap us out of our trance-like state suddenly to discover the open space of total freedom, joy, and unconditional love, a state that has always been present but has gone unnoticed.

I have personally found that all the answers we seek lie within our own consciousness and inner wisdom. That which we are seeking is already fully present within. We only need to know how to access that rich treasury of wisdom, happiness, and enlightenment for ourselves. The methods of direct access are what this book offers to share. The application of the methods I discuss easily bring recognition of our own intrinsic *Natural Bliss of Being*. The methods as generically presented, I call the Way of Light for reasons you'll discover in the chapters that follow. In discovering our "true nature" we discover an inner realm that is grounded in joy, wisdom, and unconditional love. In actualizing and empowering our "true life," we bring benefit to all.

I would like to share some unexplainable experiences I had in Saudi Arabia and in the foothills of the Himalayas in northern India, in a land known as the Vale of Kashmir. It was in these ancient and mystical places that I first encountered certain revelations from a dimension of which I had no previous knowledge. I experienced firsthand what many only read about in stories, often second or third hand. It was these and other experiences that I will share that fueled the dynamics of my further research, which eventually culminated in the writing of this book.

Chapter One

Revelations from the Unseen

We were driving back through the desert to the city of Riyadh in Saudi Arabia. About 120 miles of flat highway surrounded by desert sands and dunes would be our vista for the next two hours or so. This was during the fall of 1977. It wouldn't be so bad other than the fact that the scenery was so repetitive and the temperature was around 125 degrees Fahrenheit outside the car and around 95 degrees inside the late-model Buick, even with the air conditioning on full blast. We had just completed a lunch meeting at a farm of a wealthy Saudi landowner who was interested in doing business with our company. At that time we offered expertise in hydroponic agricultural irrigation systems. It was around three p.m. on a very hot day, yet a typical temperature for that time of year.

My Saudi business associate, Omar, was driving. I sat in the front passenger seat and the president and owner of the US company with which I worked sat in the rear seat with his cowboy hat drawn over his eyes. I was definitely overdressed, clad in a three-piece suit with tie. Even though the air conditioner was on and functioning at full capacity, it felt as though I was riding in a portable dry sauna. I laid my head back on the headrest hoping I would drop off to sleep in an effort to escape my increasing discomfort. No luck. I was just too uncomfortable to drift off. So I just sat quietly with my eyes closed.

Suddenly a dreamlike vision appeared as though I was seeing a movie projected inside my forehead, appearing in the area between my eyes and slightly above. My eyes were closed. The lighting in the vision was noticeably different from ordinary perception. It was as though the environment was self-illuminated, everything glowing from within and very clear with sharp focus of detailing.

I saw a long black ribbon extending across a distant horizon, as though I was riding on the ribbon as it extended out into the distance in front of me. I soon realized this was a black asphalt road extending out across a desert. I noticed a white form heading directly toward me from the other direction. As it got closer, I began to observe greater detail of this approaching white object. It was obviously a small pickup truck moving rapidly in my direction. As it came within fifty yards, I could see the driver. He appeared to be a dark-skinned Arab with a red checkered headdress or bandana on his head. His vehicle was coming closer, clearly traveling at a high rate of speed.

Suddenly the driver's head slumped over the steering wheel and his truck lurched wildly across the center line directly in front of my line of vision. The vehicle veered across to the other side of the highway but fortunately barely missed the front of our vehicle. Now on my right side, it rolled over three times and came to rest upright against a wire mesh fence. The driver stumbled from his vehicle, his left elbow bleeding profusely on his white cotton robe. He supported himself by clinging to the mesh fence with his hands. He turned and looked directly at me as our eyes met for a brief moment.

At that moment my body jerked suddenly, as one sometimes does when dreaming of falling, and I opened my eyes to see Omar looking at me curiously. I told him what I just saw and that I was not asleep but totally captivated by what appeared to be some kind of visionary perception. As I spoke about seeing the white vehicle coming closer and closer, I noticed a vehicle coming directly toward us. I paused in describing my "vision" only to notice the vehicle rapidly approaching was a small white truck with an Arab driver wearing some kind of red bandana. He slumped over the wheel as though he had just fallen asleep, his vehicle veering directly in front us, just barely avoiding a high-speed head-on collision. Omar slammed on the brakes and froze. The white truck rolled over three times and came to rest next to a wire mesh fence. The driver staggered out and grabbed the fence for support, exposing a bloody left elbow. He turned and looked over his shoulder directly at me, making eye contact.

Since we were stopped in the middle of a highway where every-one drove at very high speeds, I knew we had to pull off the road immediately. Omar had frozen completely, having just missed an almost certain rendezvous with death. I grabbed the steering wheel from Omar and told him to accelerate, which allowed us to pull off the road almost instantly. We certainly would have been rear-ended otherwise. My boss in the back seat was startled from his nap and yelled out in his Colorado western drawl, "What the hell is going on?" At that point I was excitedly explaining to both of them that I just saw what happened almost two minutes before it happened, and it happened *exactly* as I had seen previously in my vision.

I further explained quite excitedly that we just missed dying in a head-on collision. The three of us sat there momentarily stunned, not saying a word. Other cars pulled off the road and began offering the injured driver aid. We thought it was better for us just to proceed along our way, not knowing what sort of legal complications could ensue, and so we did.

I was completely stunned by this entire experience, to say the least. What are the implications? Is there a future world we can tap into? Has everything already "happened"? Or perhaps our limited minds are caught in three-dimensional space-time, where we are limited to experiencing reality as seeming to roll out in a linear and sequential chronology. Are we perceiving only snippets or slivers of a timeless reality that we label as "now"? Stephen Hawking suggested in his book *A Brief History of Time* that all of reality—past, present, and future—is contained in one giant hyper-sphere. Everything is complete already. Everything has already happened, and we could theoretically explore and experience any point within this hyper-sphere of total reality.

Louis de Broglie, an early quantum physicist, suggested that we could imagine all of reality as a giant pie and our limited, finite consciousness as a knife that cuts through the pie. Our conscious experience is "slicing" through the pie, as seen through the cutting blade of our awareness, while passing through one particular cut of the pie or reality known as our "life" experience. There may be many other explanations possible, but whatever the explanation for true clairvoyant experiences, we must be open to the possibility that this phenomena *does* actually happen. For me, there was no doubt at all, as I was in the process of explaining my clairvoyant vision when the actual event took place within two minutes of the vision. There was not much time for the mind to massage the story to fit some imaginary "believed" clairvoyant experience. It was captured raw and unprocessed.

Later on, I had the good fortune of being in the business of international real estate investment, which allowed me to travel extensively across the world. Often when I was in some opportune location like India, Nepal, Japan, China, or the Middle East, I would find the time to visit masters or teachers of different spiritual traditions who I felt could offer further guidance and insight regarding my spiritual search. So the real questions that begged further insight were: Is there a God or "higher power" that is the intelligence behind all of apparent creation? Is it possible to experience or know this higher power within ourselves? How can I best realize and actualize my most essential true spiritual nature? Of course, I had many other questions as well that would find their expression throughout the many discussions I had with the various masters and teachers I had met. But ultimately, the message was the same in all cases: the answers that I sought were to be found only within my own inner treasury of gnosis and wisdom. That message in itself was a pointer of great significance because it made clear that we all have a reservoir of great wisdom and enlightenment within our own being. Teachers can only direct us how to look within our *own* resources in order to discover that which we seek.

Prior to the clairvoyant event I described above, I was on a business trip to Saudi Arabia earlier in 1977. Between business meetings in Riyadh, I had a break for two weeks. I decided to visit India, Kashmir. I had never been there but had seen pictures of a place called the Vale of Kashmir, revealing it to be one of the most beautiful and mysterious places on earth. I arranged through a travel agency to buy an airline ticket through New Delhi to Srinagar in Kashmir. The next day I boarded a flight from Riyadh to New Delhi, making a connection to Srinagar. I made no hotel arrangements, as I wanted to just arrive and spontaneously let things evolve in their own way. My style was one that always allowed ample opportunity for unexpected adventure at the risk of convenience and predictability, and so it was the same on the occasion of arriving at the airport in Srinagar. The scene was total chaos as I appeared in the arrival area with checked bags in hand. Various individuals offered lodging on handwritten signs held above their heads to attract the newly arrived visitor's attention. It was common that visitors not staying at regular hotels stayed on floating houseboats that could have as many as six sleeping cabins. One young man managed to catch my eye with his enthusiastic sign waving for a houseboat called the Kashmir Paradise. He immediately came up and offered to take my bag, stating that his family had one of the most beautiful houseboats on Dal Lake. His name was Ali Baktoo, and his father owned the Kashmir

Paradise houseboat. He spoke excellent English and was friendly and knowledgeable regarding the area and what it had to offer. I agreed to stay on his family's houseboat, and we set out from the airport in his car.

When we arrived at the shore line docks, he took my bag and brought us to a very long thin canoe called a shikara. We boarded the shikara for a short journey to the houseboat. This canoe was the skinniest boat I had ever been on, and I was amazed that we were able to keep balance. It had practically no sides and was almost flush with the water. Miraculously, after about ten minutes, we arrived completely dry at the hotel on the water, known proudly by Ali's family as the Kashmir Paradise. We entered the main living room of the houseboat where I found a comfortable chair to relax in. The decorations were a combination of Victorian English and traditional Indian styles. It felt as though I was sitting in a British parlor awaiting traditional afternoon tea around the time of the British Raj. Nonetheless, I was comfortable in my surroundings, especially considering that I could see the lake and surrounding Himalayan Mountains from the open windows quite easily.

Ali told me it would be a while before my room was ready and that he would go into the village for food supplies. He asked if I had any special requests. I remember asking if it was true that there were holy men in the mountains who were spiritually enlightened and if he knew of anyone in the nearby villages he could arrange for me to meet with. He told me indeed that there were Sufis who lived in the area who were known to have miraculous spiritual powers. Sufis are Islamic mystics who have attained a high level of spiritual enlightenment through the special yogic exercises and meditation practices of their tradition. The relationship of Sufism to Islam is very much analogous to the relationship of Kabbalah to Orthodox Judaism. Both traditions are the inner esoteric crown jewels of their respective exoteric religions. Mystics of both traditions, Sufism and Kabbalah, have been known for centuries to have communicated with and experienced the highest spiritual realities. In Sufism, these experiences have been captured in poetry and prose by such great Sufi mystics as Rumi, Omar Khayyam, Hafez, Shabistari, Ibn Al Arabi, and Al Ghazali to mention some of the most famous.

I made myself comfortable in the parlor until Ali had returned with the supplies. After about two hours, he appeared with several bags of provisions, and behind him stood an elderly gentleman dressed meagerly in loincloth-like shorts and a tattered blue shirt. He had a long white beard that stood out in contrast to his otherwise tawny and browned skin. On his head was fashioned a rather tawdry white turban. I remember clearly though, his penetrating light blue eyes that sat deeply in his eye sockets staring out at mine. I was sitting on the other side of the room. He walked across the room with the authority of a doctor about to examine a patient. He peered over my shoulders and head as he pulled back my collar exposing my neck and upper back to his gaze. He looked down the back of my shirt and gazed at my back for twenty seconds, or so and then released my shirt and took a sitting position on the floor a few feet in front of my chair. He was sitting on the floor with his knees together in front and his feet facing to the rear. He began speaking without having asked me any questions regarding myself or my history. Ali began to translate, as the man was not able to speak English. He spoke a Persian dialect known as Urdu, the typical language of the Muslim population of the region.

He leaned forward, rubbed his knees in a circular fashion, and began speaking. He said that there was a woman with whom I lived in the United States who had great pain in both of her knees and that it was a most unfortunate situation. The hair on my neck stood on end as the meaning of his words sunk in. My girlfriend, with whom I lived in Los Angeles, had just had double knee surgery shortly before I left for Europe and Saudi Arabia. She actually had surgery on both knees for congenital dislocating patella.

In laymen's terms, her knees sometimes dislocated, causing her horrendous pain. She had casts on both legs from her ankles almost to her hips for several weeks. Fortunately, we had friends who offered care and support, which allowed me to leave on this long-planned business trip. This Sufi sitting in front of me had no way to know any of this; I had not shared any of my private life with anyone including Ali since arriving. What were the odds that he could have guessed such a situation? How many people do you know that have significant pain in both knees at the same time that are young and vital? I was twenty-seven at the time and my girlfriend was twenty-five. If this was just a guess on his part, he sure made an amazing guess!

In the next minutes, as he continued sitting on the floor, he spoke again. Ali was translating. While he rubbed his lower stomach he said, "This same poor woman several months before had great pain in her lower stomach. It caused her great distress, and it was a very grave situation." At hearing these words I knew this man had some special power of insight without doubt. Several months earlier, Linda alerted me one evening that she was feeling serious pain in the area of her uterus. Because she was pregnant, we were extremely concerned. It got so bad, that we decided to rush her to the hospital. I drove her to Queen of Angels hospital, near where we lived in Los Angeles. They rushed her into the emergency room where they determined she was having a miscarriage and was bleeding internally. They performed a procedure to stop the bleeding and informed us that the baby had not survived. It was quite a traumatic time for us both, but at least Linda was safe and free of the agonizing pain.

No doubt, this Sufi seer had accessed information that was beyond human ability to know. He had access to another level of reality that allowed him to know things that others couldn't possibly know. I was so shocked by his few spoken words, which were so profoundly descriptive of events and feelings that were impossible for him to know.

I recovered my composure and immediately asked him if he would be willing to accept me as a student within his Sufi tradition. He made it clear that he does not have students, as he has nothing to teach anyone. He said his power comes from Allah as a gift, and he cannot give that gift to another. But there was a Sufi master in the region that has students, and I should arrange to meet with him. He said I needed to meet with Pir Qassim Qadria. Ali told me he would make the necessary arrangements.

As the man was about to leave, I offered him some money for his time. He said emphatically that he could not accept money for his gifts. He said that his gifts come from Allah and that if he took money, he would certainly lose his connection with Allah. He wished me well and proceeded to return to his village.

From both of these encounters, the Sufi clairvoyant in Kashmir and my own clairvoyant experience in the desert of Arabia, it became clear that there is another level of consciousness available to us. These encounters with clairvoyance permanently altered my view of reality and our possible experience within the universe.

The next day, Ali made arrangements for me to visit the Sufi teacher Qassim, who was well known in the region. The following day we went by taxi for about two hours to meet and visit with Qassim in Anantanag. He was very gracious and most willing to answer all my questions. He explained the methods of Sufi practice and gave me written instructions for the meditations. He explained the Sufi system of inner meditation on energy centers within the body, heart, and mind. Through doing these meditation practices one's consciousness is eventually transformed into a sublime spiritual state in which one could fathom the mysteries of Being, as well as the nature and meaning of human existence firsthand. This was in perfect alignment with my own spiritual quest.

After spending several days with Qassim, he decided to take me to visit the place where his Sufi master was buried. It was far out in nature, in the mountains of the Hindu Kush, near a small stream. After spending several minutes reverently by the small grave, we proceeded up the side of a very steep mountain among very tall and dense pine trees. We were with a small group of his disciples, about ten of us in total. I found it hard to believe that Qassim, who was overweight, would be able to negotiate his way up the steep trail leading to his mountain hut. But he made it successfully up the several hundred yards to the hut.

It was set completely in the depth of a pine forest. There was no road leading there. When we got inside everyone proceeded to find a place to sit as Qassim asked, through my translator, what exactly I would like to know. I told him that I would like to have direct experience of God. He then directed that I walk over to one of his students sitting across the room. He told me to look into his eyes and to tell him what I saw. I told him that I only saw his face and eyes. He then said in a very matter-of-fact way, "You are seeing God, looking at God." A sudden recognition occurred along with a moment of total stillness of mind—just silence. The silence began to evolve into realizations of understanding that melted away all sense of duality, such as God "out there" and me "in here." God became more intimate than my own idea of myself.

> *"What we are looking for, is what's looking."*
> *St. Francis of Assisi*

From my earlier years in Zen Buddhism and other spiritual paths, my notion of God was not that of a "creator God" who stood apart from us and creation, but rather that God was the core of our own Being within. The Sufis have the same notion but are bound by the language and theology of Judeo-Christian-based Islam. For a Sufi, total spiritual illumination has often been expressed in such terms as "I am God" or "I am He," where the personality of the Sufi has dissolved into the Presence of Divine Being. Sufis have had to keep this mystical experience to themselves, having learned tragic lessons when other Sufis publicly shared their epiphany. They were usually executed for heresy by the conservative Muslim clergy. One of the Desert Fathers of early Christianity, as I mentioned in the introduction, said "To know one's self is to know God." So this mystical experience was not just the province of the Sufis.

Little did I know that this was just a prelude to much deeper insights and illuminations that would arise as I began my Sufi meditation practices after arriving back in the United States. But before I returned to the United States, Qassim and I spent time together, which gave me the opportunity to ask more questions and clarify what I had already learned. He gave me a Sufi name, Latif Qadria. *Latif* means "the most subtle quality of God's presence," one of the ninety-nine names of God. To Sufis the name Latif refers to the subtle inner energy body that is the active divine energy within our souls. He told me whenever I wished to speak with him or he wished to contact me that he would appear in dreams or visions while I was meditating. That turned out to be a rather auspicious and foreboding discussion.

A couple of days after I returned home to the U.S., I was sleeping one night and had a very unusual dream. I was in India, perhaps Kashmir, walking down a dusty dirt road leading to a small village. In the middle of the road was a large round well, obviously used by people coming to fetch water. Behind the well, coming from the distance, I saw a figure walking in my direction. It was Qassim. As he was getting closer, he telepathically communicated a troubling message.

He said, "Latif, I bring you a message of death. But don't be worried or concerned as it doesn't affect you or anyone very close to you."

As he said those words, I heard a ringing sound that was out of place for the dream environment. I immediately awoke to the sound of my home phone ringing. The phone was in the room below our bedroom, the kitchen. I jumped out of bed to go answer the phone as I thought because of the hour, around six a.m., it may be an important call. It was my girlfriend's mother. She was in Chicago, at O'Hare airport waiting to board a flight to London. At the time, we were living in Colorado. She said she had just gotten word that her mother was dying and she needed to get to the hospital as soon as possible. She told me to tell her daughter, Carolyn, that she was leaving and not to worry. Carolyn was still sleeping upstairs. When I returned upstairs, Carolyn asked me who had called and I explained the situation regarding her mother and grandmother. But I told her the most amazing thing was that I was just in a dream with Qassim telling me that he was bringing me a "message of death" when the phone rang. She was astounded as well but not sure what to make of the whole thing.

These events gave me further certainty that there was an "unseen" world of spiritual realities that lie beyond our wildest imagination but not beyond our wildest dreams. I was being pulled deeper again into this profound depth of perception that I believed most of us would only know after death. How is it that some are able to navigate in both worlds, our material world of limitation and another that seems to exist outside the conventions of space and time?

I was further encouraged to explore this new spiritual vista that became ever clearer within the eye of my heart. It's been more than thirty-five years since my first experiences as described in Saudi Arabia and the Vale of Kashmir. Since that time, I have had many opportunities to study with Tibetan Lamas in Nepal and Zen masters in China, Korea, and Japan. I also studied other traditions under the tutelage of teachers in those lineages. But most importantly, I put their teachings and instructions to practical application within my own meditation practice. Coming to a deep understanding and profound insight about what these teachings convey allows me to share a path that I believe anyone can follow.

The essential insights are not complex at all, but there is a necessity to understand the map that describes the territory that's the basis of our journey. I believe the path begins with an understanding of how our minds operate and how thought impacts our well-being on every level—physical, emotional, social, and spiritual.

Chapter Two

Understanding the Mind and the Nature of Enlightenment

We are what we think. All that we are arises with our thoughts. With our thoughts, we make our world.
—The Buddha,
from the Dhammapada

Since this book focuses on the topic of enlightenment, it's probably best if we begin by defining the word *enlightenment*. There are many definitions to choose from, depending on the tradition or culture discussed. For our purposes, we will use the definitions that are associated most with Buddhism, Hinduism, and Eastern philosophy in general. Enlightenment as a word is best described by understanding the meanings contained within the word itself: a condition wherein light has been brought to a topic or state of mind. In this case, *light* refers to insight, understanding, or wisdom. For our purposes, enlightenment means a profound and deep insight that has illuminated our sense of who we are in the grand scheme of things, spiritually, morally and socially. Along with this enlightenment comes a freedom from the darkness of not knowing who we are, which is discovered to be the reason for our suffering, sense of personal alienation, and general discontent. Another term for enlightenment is appropriately known as *self-realization*. We come to realize who and what we actually are.

Most of us seek happiness and fulfillment through relationships, achievements, and acquisitions. Yet we never seem to find any lasting stability in our quest. It is this unending quest that Eastern traditions have described by the word *samsara*, which invokes an image of "running around in circles" like a hamster on a wheel that goes faster and faster but gets nowhere. Ultimately this effort only produces more suffering and dissatisfaction. We run around everywhere in pursuit of happiness and fulfillment but we fail to ponder the possibility that what we seek is already fully complete within ourselves. This is not to say in an egotistical way, "Oh boy! I have everything I need within myself!" but rather to say "Oh my, who I thought I was now includes everyone and everything!" This occurs through a shift in personal identity, from being a defined and limited "self" to being an undefined, living matrix of possibility and interdependent wholeness. By this recognition, a natural joy and sense of oneness with creation abides that seems to be energized by existence itself.

We discover that our suffering and discontent was not based on a failure to attain what we desired but rather on not understanding the "seeker." When we don't know who we are in relationship to life in its broadest definition, we try to assuage that existential angst or sense of separateness by engendering a continuous stream of ego gratifications to distract us from our basic dilemma. For some, great success in the game of ego gratification attends, but at some point when a person feels he or she "has it all," the game no longer acts as a distraction. The person feels an existential emptiness in all he or she has "achieved."

Again, the cause of our suffering is not our failures regarding life's challenges but in not understanding who we are and what our relationship to life is. There is no doubt that we exist in some fashion, but there is a lot of doubt about whom and what we are.

We create many self-definitions for ourselves beginning in our earliest years. We are influenced by these self-images often for the rest of our lives. The self that we *consider* we are is made up wholly of our thoughts. In life we may suffer all kinds of con-ditioning experiences, yet the way those experiences affect us is determined by our thoughts regarding them. There is also the possibility that there is an authentic spiritual beingness within us. That state of spiritual beingness has profound meaning exis-tentially. However, there simultaneously exists our imagined self, constructed wholly of thoughts reflective of our conditioning. The latter is called the ego in psychology and common usage. The for-mer is what is revealed in enlightenment. The difference between the two is only a thought away.

To clarify, our sense of self is a product of our thoughts. So if our suffering and general discontent in life is caused by our false and imagined thoughts regarding our sense of self, then it would seem wise to fully understand the nature of thought and its power to benefit or harm our general sense of well-being. Indeed, the Eastern traditions came to the same conclusion more than three thousand years ago. The masters of the great traditions teach that the gateway to enlightenment begins with understanding the nature of thought. And so we must enter through the same gate if we intend to arrive at the same destination: enlightenment and freedom from personal suffering.

Many excellent teachers today point out the importance of seeing through our thoughts and to disbelieve the messages they offer, especially negative thoughts. Others talk about lib-erating ourselves from the endless stories that our minds weave through thought, imagination, and belief, causing anxiety and emotional suffering. This is often taught as learning to *not believe* what our thoughts are telling us, especially the negative thoughts that create anxiety, worry, and depressed emotional states. This is great advice to be sure, and all of us need to be cognizant of how we depress ourselves or create anxiety through our own apparently volitional, thought processes. We often dwell on potential negative future outcomes or irreparable events from the past with regret and shame. To learn that we can liberate ourselves from uncomfortable emotional states through recognizing our negative thinking patterns is invaluable. But before we can think in terms of liberating ourselves from negative emotional states, we first have to understand their origin.

As the Buddha pointed out correctly two thousand five hundred years ago, what we are is the result of our thoughts. Some have said we are the result of our experiences, but I would add that we are the result of what we think *about* our experiences. So that means that how we are feeling, our current emotional state, is dictated by our thoughts. If that's true, then we need to find this out for ourselves. The best way to do that is to examine the nature of our thoughts.

So that we are able to remain "on the same page" regarding the topic of thoughts, I suggest that we engage in the brief exercises that follow. Don't just read the exercises, but play with them a bit. I am not trying to convey a dry conceptual understanding of the mind but rather invite a true investigation into the topic directly. Through this investigation, certain insights will become the foundation of an experiential understanding necessary to appreciate what follows in later chapters.

Take a moment and just notice your thoughts as they pass through your mind. Take the perspective that you are looking into the sky watching the clouds drift by. In this case, the clouds drifting by are your thoughts passing through your awareness.

Don't judge the thoughts or get caught up in their stories, just observe what appears and disappears in your mind.

We may be able to notice that there are two significant aspects present in our experience: (1) the thoughts observed and (2) the conscious observer of those thoughts. The observer notices the clouds drift by. Thoughts come and go, but this observing quality seems stationary as the observer. We could also use the analogy of a mirror and its reflections: As the observer of your thoughts, you are like the mirror. The thoughts are like the reflections. So again, take a few minutes this time and just observe your thoughts as they appear, as though you are a mirror with no vested interest in whatever reflections appear.

Now this time instead of focusing on the thoughts, focus on *you* as the observer. There are the events of the mind and the *observer* of them. Take a few moments and notice this observing quality in your mind. It might help if you sense that your awareness is located just behind the eyes. Your awareness is the *seeing* that takes in your visionary perceptions. In daylight or in a well-lit room, close your eyes and put your attention on the inside of your eyelids. Notice the outer light shining on your eyelids makes for an inner view of an orangey-red shade of light. Try to gain a sense of where you are in regard to this light. You may feel you are a few inches in back of your eyes looking forward at the light, or you may seem right up in the light, or you may be further back in your head looking forward at the light from a distance.

Is there any distance between you as the observer and the light experienced?

Whatever your experience, at least you have the clear sense of being an observer and that which is observed, the light. Next, let's switch the object observed from the light to a thought. With your eyes closed, get a mental picture of a dog in your mind. Notice the dog and your sense of being the observer of the image.

Bring your attention on yourself as the observer, and notice what happens to the image of the dog. When you shift your attention to your subjective perspective as the viewer, the image of the dog either fades or disappears. Inversely, the more you focus on the details of the dog, your sense of being the observer fades. Using this principle you can find relief when troubled by a particular thought or worry. Observe your troubling thought, and then switch your attention to yourself as the observer—the witness— of the thought. Switch your attention several times from the subjective witness-noticing-the-witness position to the witness-noticing-the-thought position. This should relieve most of the intensity of any associated discomfort. This method also works with emotional states.

Hopefully you have noticed this "observing" quality that perceives your thoughts and perceptions to be at the position from which you are looking. The remaining portions of this book explore that observing quality of the mind, its true nature, and how it relates to spiritual enlightenment. You will learn that the observing consciousness is not dependent on your thoughts, emotions, feelings, sensory perceptions, or sense of identity for its existence. It is of a different dimension, and it is your true and unchanging spiritual nature. You are always you, the unchanging, observing knowingness in all experience.

Let's take another look within our minds again: For this exercise, you remain exactly where you are or find a quiet space to sit, free of distraction. Again notice your state of mind, the thoughts and images passing in front of your awareness. See if you can notice an occasional gap free of thoughts between the disappearance of one thought and before the next one appears. This gap may last one or two seconds, but it can be observed. Take a few moments until you have noticed an empty space where there is no thought appearing. Once you have managed that, do it again, this time noticing how the observer remains whether there is a thought present or not. Work on this for several minutes if necessary, until it becomes clear that, as an unchanging observer, you are present whether thoughts appear or are absent.

The entire pursuit of spiritual traditions that consider enlightenment as their goal is the clarification of what this observer or aware quality of the mind is all about. Some questions to consider: Is the observer of thoughts a thought itself? Is this observing awareness a function of the brain, or is it something that exists independent of the body and brain? Since it can observe thoughts as though independent and separate from thoughts, does that mean this observing awareness is not conditioned by the mind's activities?

By reviewing and repeating the above exercises with these questions in mind, it may be possible to gain a greater experiential and intuitive insight into the nature of consciousness and being. We need to realize that we are that observing awareness; we are not the observed thoughts or images.

As we examine the nature of this awareness we find no fixed qualities other than this capacity to observe. It's always in the now, observing. Even when we are engaged in memories, that which is observing the memories of "then" is in the current moment of now. We sometimes say that when we are engaged in a memory, our mind is absorbed in the past. But the memory is occurring now, as a freshly created mental image based on past experience, and the observer of that memory is always in the present. We can also notice that quality of changeless observing when regarding thoughts of the future. Awareness is always in this current moment; there is no other option.

The unchanging, observing awareness is present not only as the perceiver of thoughts and mental phenomena but also as the perceiving awareness of sensory and perceptual experiences of the "outer world." Within our embodied existence, we have five senses. What we don't recognize is the nature of those five senses.

The experience of the five senses is always free from our conditioning, thoughts, and stories. Direct perceptual experience, which always precedes our thoughts and labeling regarding those perceptions, is itself pure and innocent of description. However, in the following micro-second the mind interprets meaning and definition. Notice while looking at what you are seeing: your thoughts have no effect on the colors and textures of raw perceptual, visual input. Next notice the same thing with what you are hearing. The same is true for all physical sensations, including taste and smell. So what is in your mind has no effect on the *functioning* of the five senses. The five senses are there by default, without requiring the mind's permission, just like your skin.

Another factor of consciousness that is present in perceptual experience is the observer of experience, which we have been discussing. Someone or something is aware of the raw perceptual experience of the five senses. Let's call it *awareness*. It is our observer from previous discussions, the observing knowingness that you actually are. This awareness doesn't occur after the fact, like the thinking mind; it is present in the first perceptual moment of experience. So it is not the mind or thoughts, it is also pre-mind. And what we mean by mind are the functions of thinking, memory, and imagination. This witnessing awareness also is present when the mind is evaluating and interpreting perceptions as they occur. And it continues to be present after thinking and perceptions have ceased as well. In total stillness of mind, awareness is still aware—aware of the "still state." So we can safely conclude that awareness is not dependent on the mind, thoughts, or mental images. Like the five senses, awareness is there by default, just like the marrow of your bones.

The more we remain in the awareness mode of just observing inner and outer phenomena, the more a sense and certainty of *being* arises. The unchanging nature of awareness is a state of being. It is our calm and quiet corner. It is our true unchanging beingness, the same generic sense of being we had as young children, teenagers, young adults, and who we are today. When we look back at our earliest years, it seems we have never *not* been ourselves. Who else could we be? We may have all sorts of self-definitions regarding who we believe we are, but there is still an underlying sense of just being someone as an existing conscious presence that doesn't change over time. Many elderly people have shared that they feel they are the same person as when they were young. Our roles may change, but the awareness that is experiencing those roles does not. Undefined *beingness* has a permanent quality of awareness. If we recognize fully what that beingness is, in all its spiritual ramifications, and as seen from that perspective, we would be enlightened.

Most basic is our sense of existing as a being. That quality of being or existing does not appear to depend on anything material in terms of how we look, feel, or act. It also isn't affected by our mind or how we think of ourselves. The phrase "I think, therefore I am" does not reveal what precedes the thinking. We don't know we exist simply because we think; we know we exist because we are aware. Thinking is no more a validation of existence than the five perceptual senses. So thinking is not the proof. The *awareness* that we are thinking, feeling, or perceiving is our proof of being. Awareness is more fundamental. To be is to be aware. To be aware is to be. Awareness is intrinsic to our being.

If we spend any time contemplating or just noticing our mental processes we may notice that in moments of stillness, free of thoughts, there is a naked and clear sense of aware beingness. From that basic sense of being we easily notice that it is always aware. We also notice that there appears to be a power of attention with which we create the style of our experience. For example, we can direct our attention to negative thoughts, and by focusing further on negative thoughts we develop negative moods and emotions. We can also focus our attention on positive thoughts and experience positive moods and emotions. Attention is a power of awareness. The power of attention reaches into the physical world of experience too. By focusing our attention on achieving some goal in life we actualize that initial thought into reality. Literally all that we achieve through effort in life is directed by our power of attention.

So, *being* has the quality of awareness. Awareness has the power of attention. Attention then is the conduit of *intention*, which is the creative pulse that arises from being and enlivens the creative process of living in the world. Intention first manifests as thought, the idea to be intended. Action arises from the intention to do something.

It's important to get a handle on understanding the nature of our intentions. Often our suffering is caused by intending to resist some aspect of reality or life situation. We create our own suffering by intending things to be different than they are. We then become frustrated by our intentions not coming to fruition. We feel let down or depressed by things not turning out the way we intended. Our entire day is "run" by intention. A profitable endeavor could be to question yourself throughout the day about your intentions. For example, notice how many emotional states are related to the intentions we generate. Clarity on this topic can bring great relief when we realize exactly what we are creating for ourselves by our intentions. In fact, our entire world view, positive or negative, is based on our thoughts and intentions. Keeping that in mind, let's look at what is *noticing* these intentions and thoughts.

Take a moment and look at your thoughts and intentions as they arise and fade away. In the moment of noticing the thought, suddenly place your attention on yourself as the observing awareness. What happened to the thought or intention when you suddenly focused on you, the observer? If you work with this a bit, you notice that when you successfully place your attention on yourself as the observing awareness, the thought vanishes, just as we noticed earlier with the image of the dog. This is a key to what is known as the *self-liberation of thoughts* in certain Tibetan Buddhist meditation traditions. Through this method we release ourselves from emotional and psychological sufferings. The most important element to this method is the power of attention. We shift our attention to this pure observing quality of awareness that is the observer or knower of our thoughts. By releasing the attention from the thought, it is no longer being energized. Our attention sustains our thoughts, stories, and emotional states.

Let's outline how to apply this practically. For example: sit on a comfortable chair or cushion on the floor. Close your eyes and recall the feeling of anger. As you experience this feeling of anger, observe the emotion and how your body feels. After a short while, bring your attention to your awareness that is observing the feeling of anger. Anger is the *object* of observation and your awareness is the viewing *subject*. You are switching your attention from the object to the subject. Notice what changes as you do this. In most cases, the anger subsides or disappears. As you gain proficiency with this, try it again, but this time with the feeling of sadness. Then try it with the feeling of fear. Then try anxiety. Think about what emotional states seem to be most challenging in your life experience, then do the exercise with each one. Hopefully by engaging in this practice you can succeed with actual life experiences of negative emotional states as they arise. The lesson ultimately is that by simply remaining in the condition of being a detached observer to negative emotional states as they first arise, you won't become your own victim.

So let's summarize the overall process being discussed.

First, there is *being*. We notice being is aware and, through the mind's functions, has the power of attention and intention.

From the intention to conceptualize, thoughts arise. We then further energize those thoughts by keeping attention on them. That's how we create stories in our mind and generate action in our lives. It is also the mechanism that causes suffering to persist, which is the mind's continued enlivening of negative thoughts by giving them attention. Without the mind's continuing attention, those thoughts vanish. This is also true of particular thoughts called problems. Problems only exist in our heads. There are no problems existing in the universe. You may look all you wish but you will never find a problem "out there" because all problems exist only "in here." That's not to say that there aren't situations demanding someone's attention in our daily lives. But those situations only become a problem when noticed and then thought about. It's the *thinking about it* that is the problem, not the situation. It's the *thinking about* it that creates stress, not the situation.

What if instead of placing our attention on our thoughts, we simply left our attention to rest passively within awareness as attentive alertness or empty presence, like a young child staring at some fascinating scene? We simply remain in the total openness and presence of observing awareness. As the tendency to compulsively enter thinking-mode diminishes, you no longer need to focus your attention in order to remain within thought-free awareness. Attention becomes like a well-trained dog that obediently sits at its master's feet awaiting the next direction to act. In most of the Buddhist teachings such as Zen and certain Tibetan traditions, this passive but vividly alert "resting and relaxing of attention within awareness" is the practice. It's not enlightenment, but it is the context in which much deeper realizations and insights develop and arise spontaneously. As this practice becomes stable, you simply continue in and *as* this natural observingness. When in this relaxed condition the mind is clear, attentive, and open. You feel a spacious and transparent quality of being that is both serene and highly responsive to the needs of your environmental and personal relationships.

Question: What is a thought?

Answer: Thought is mental energy with a message, like a momentary cloud with writing on it. Essentially, it's semitransparent information. The information may point to something relevant or it may be useless distraction. In either case it has no actual substance. By focusing our attention on it, it becomes more solid. When left alone it fades and subsides on its own.

Question: What if my mind is so full of thoughts that I can't notice a separate observer standing apart from thoughts?

Answer: At times this is the case for everyone. When you are so full of thoughts it is sometimes better to focus on the body or sensory experience instead of the mind. I recommend focusing on your breathing. While sitting or lying, just focus on noticing the experience of the breath passing through the nostrils and then follow how the breath fills the lungs. As the in-breath is at its natural fullness, notice how it begins to exit through the nostrils and the sensations when the chest begins to empty and relax. As you exhale, slow the breath down and lengthen the exhalation into full relaxation. Pause before inhaling again. During the pause, notice the experience of relaxation for a brief moment. Then start the cycle again. Do this for about five minutes or until you feel more relaxed. Then practice the "observing thoughts exercise" again.

Question: Is the goal of these practices to get rid of all thoughts and thinking?

Answer: No, not at all. Thoughts are the natural expression of the mind. However, most of us don't notice how we create our own uncomfortable states of mind through our apparently volitional thinking process. We blame the environment or the people around us. We completely miss our own involvement through thinking, judging, and attempting to manipulate our world to be as we prefer. However, as we become more and more aware of our natural condition as being this observing awareness, we are less identified with our thoughts automatically. Since we are more developed in the mode of being an observer of inner and external experiences, thoughts appear less contracted and solid. We can begin to see through the haze of our thoughts and stories. We notice our sensory perceptions to be more vivid and alive. Colors appear more intense and sounds seem crisper. Its not that our senses are functioning any better, but our attention is relaxing into a state of non-fixated openness. As we relax into this new openness more and more, the mind's frenetic activities begin to slow down, and eventually a natural stillness of mind may arise. A creative and playful intuitiveness arises that seems to replace much of the compulsive think-and- worry mode that we experience so often. It is this carefree state of mind that makes living fun and less "effortful." Life seems to flow without needing to be forced one way or another.

Question: Is there a method or application of what you have been sharing here that can help reduce an overall sense of restlessness and discontent?

Answer: All of the various causes of discontent and restlessness are caused by our beliefs as embodied in our thoughts. Imagine in this moment if all your beliefs about everything vanished suddenly and your mind became thought-free. Since your mind is thought-free, you couldn't have any worries or problems in mind. You would have no concept of relative or absolute. You would have no concept of self or other. You would have no concept of bondage or liberation. You would have no sense of "searching." You would have no sense of "oneness" or separateness. You would have no concept of suffering or release. As long as you remained in this moment of total presence, beyond thinking-mind, nothing could disturb your sense of peace and serenity. Yet you are fully alive and alert to what's happening and you act instinctively as though engaged in dance. Your private meditation hut is fully portable and is able to be your refuge in all moments of your life. Notice how the degree to which you engage in various beliefs and stories alters the mood of the moment—from serenity to restlessness, resisting or grasping. Is there really any need to study or practice various methods when you have seen clearly how it all works? Thought-free awareness is not some lofty goal that occurs after you have mastered the art of suppressing thoughts or ignoring them. Thought-free awareness is occurring throughout the day, but we don't notice this empty space of clarity because our mind is habituated to noticing thoughts and content. Try to catch yourself in those *naturally* occurring moments of thought-free awareness. They occur when you first step in the shower and feel the water, when you first put your toothbrush into your mouth, when you have your first bite of breakfast, when you first hear a loud noise. Begin to notice those empty moments of clarity that exist between those moments of thinking and daydreaming.

The only "restlessness or discontent" you will ever know is that which results from your own thinking. *Only your own thoughts and imagination can obscure your natural state of serenity.*

Question: The way you are describing the relationship between thoughts and awareness seems dualistic. You seem to imply that awareness and thoughts are two separate independent realities. Is that correct?

Answer: It may seem that *awareness* is separate and apart from thoughts, appearances, and experiences as being an independent observer. This would be a dualistic view, a view that is counter to what all the enlightened teachers teach. But before we can know the non-duality of awareness and experience, we first need to explore our immediate experience just as it appears from our dualistic perspective. Initially we need to differentiate our observing awareness from the mind's dualistic activities as expressed through thought. This brings about a "dis-identification" of the mind's projections and its essential nature as changeless awareness. This is like the mind believing our identity is our physical body or mentally conceived self-image. We come to discover that we are not the body or psychological self-image. As we proceed, this dualistic sense of separation also gradually disappears, revealing a oneness of all and everything.

Question: What does this have to do with realizing our spiritual nature? What's the connection?

Answer: As our mind becomes less contracted into compulsive thought and worry, our space of awareness feels more open and free. Our narrow borders of self-definition begin to yield to a growing sense of connection to all of life and our world of experience. By becoming more aware of our own undefined and immaterial state of beingness, we are becoming more familiar with that aspect within ourselves that is changeless, perfect, and eternally free. The rest of this book is dedicated to bringing this knowledge into our experience.

Chapter Three

Identity, Ego, and Authentic Being

> *It is only when we have renounced our pre-occupation with "I," "me," "mine" that we can truly possess the world in which we live...provided that we regard nothing as property. And not only is everything ours, it is also everybody else's.*
> —*Aldous Huxley,*
> **The Perennial Philosophy**

All emotional suffering stems from a basic misunderstanding regarding our personal identity. This misunderstanding is expressed as erroneous thoughts that the mind comes to accept and believe. Enlightenment is the absence of any confusion as to our true identity. The mind continuously offers us suggestions and definitions of who we are. Those suggestions are mind-generated self-images and thoughts, based on conditioning and imagination. Child development studies have suggested that somewhere around fifteen to twenty-four months of age, a child begins to develop a sense of self-identity. Prior to this time, the child had no self-definition or ego. It did not have a thinking process that defined the world in terms of me, mine, and other.

Life was just an open play of sensory experience that remained unevaluated regarding any sense of self. The child also had no sense of personal ownership. Gradually through social interaction and as parents or caregivers refer to the child by name, along with other verbal cues; the child begins to infer a personal identity separate from other people and things. Through exposure to praise or negative reinforcement, the child develops a coherently biased self-image. But we need to keep in mind that this sense of self-identity is made up completely of thoughts and mental images. There is not some concrete substance called a self that suddenly appeared in the child's brain. There is only a collection of thoughts reinforced by conditioning that comprise this apparent self-identity.

This self-identity is actually just a story. But this story exists on two levels, the subconscious mind and the conscious mind. If severe emotional deficits occurred in early childhood, the child may infer that various inadequacies exist within him or herself. The child might feel like he or she does not deserve to be loved, is not good enough, or is a worthless child, to just name a few common and pernicious negative self-image issues with which many of us grow up. Unfortunately if these descriptions are implanted in the mind at an early age, they may linger for the entire life of the person. They remain as active personality schemas, or they lie dormant waiting for the appropriate external stimulus to trigger the deep-seated personal insecurities again. Our sense of self in our daily lives can be colored by these feelings and thoughts regarding self-inadequacy to such a degree that we may succumb to them. Our relationships with others fail, and our life aspirations remain unfulfilled.

The good news is that these negative self-thoughts are just thoughts. They occur in the conscious mind yet originate in the subconscious. We can also play with and create our self-images on a purely conscious level, such as when we acquire a new role in our work or personal life. We can imagine ourselves to be this or that role as we please. So a sense of self-identity does not always have to be rooted in deep psychological conditioning. The common denominator of both styles of self-identity, conscious and subconscious, is that they are both just thoughts occurring within the space of our unchanging observing awareness.

When you consciously observe the thought process in action, notice that there is always a sense of thoughts being "my thoughts." The *self* is the thinking process defining itself. *The ego-self isn't doing the thinking, but rather it is itself a thought.* The ego-self is the mind defining itself in relationship to itself and its world through thought. The feeling of personal identity is created when thinking occurs because thought is almost always polarized into a subject as me and an object as the topic of my thinking. That means that the thinking is always in regard to some self concern or issue. Also, one of the most powerful catalysts to the creation of the sense of personal identity is memory. Memory is thinking in terms of "my" past experiences, and those past experiences help shape and maintain the sense of continuous identity. Likewise visualizing myself in a future situation also gives life to the sense of personal identity and its continuity.

When trying to recover from an oppressive emotional experience, it is hard to find that relaxed sense of being a detached witness to the emotional state and its highly influential psychological messages. The experience is riveting. The reason you can't objectively observe the emotional event is that the emotional event and its subjective conceptual content is defining who we are in that moment. The sense of *me* is inseparable from the emotional reactive contraction. With that centralizing contraction in the space of thought and mind, there is a more solid sense of self. We also tense up physically when in emotional turmoil. The nature of this contraction is such that it collapses our sense of spaciousness and openness further adding to our sense of being a localized and separate entity as defined by our feelings in the experience.

For some, living in the emotional drama gives a stronger sense of identity because it is so vividly present in those moments. Though it is not a comfortable experience, it is yet *self* reinforcing. But in certain cases the energized sense of identity has more value to the mind than being free of the suffering. That's why some people thrive on turmoil and crisis. The have greater certainty or feeling that they exist. This could also be said of chronic self-pity, in which there seems to be an enjoyment within the "poor me" dynamic. Often unsuspecting customers buy a ticket to the "pity party" and find themselves sucked into someone else's needs for attention and validation. It becomes a real pity party when both start feeding off each other's unhealthy emotional needs. There are many ways that the ego structure feeds off of negative emotional states and unhealthy relationships. I recommend that you take stock of your own tendencies in this area of behavior. None of us are immune from this type of *self* reinforcing dynamic, at least not until our consciousness is no longer focused in ego-identity and has discovered timeless *beingness*, which requires no emotional reinforcement or validation.

A good practice for this situation would be to observe with objective awareness the emotional feeling along with the coexisting sense of self. This is like taking one step behind the subjective self in the experience. What is it that notices this sense of personal selfhood in distress? Seeing the entire gestalt or scenario is key. *It is seen that the impersonal observing awareness is not locked up in the event, unlike the sense of self that is.* Here we can find a sense of relief and freedom that otherwise would remain unknown.

Most of us have strong waves of emotional content that arise as the basis of our personal suffering. Instead of trying to eliminate all the causes of suffering, it is much easier to find the one panacea for all suffering: the dissolution of the illusion of imagined selfhood. It is not that we are a person who has negative emotional experiences. Rather, the *sense of being a defined person is also just an experience that arises in awareness or knowingness as a mental event.*

When we dream at night, the person that we are in the dream is not separate from the entire vignette of the dream. When the dream dissolves as we awaken, the person we were in the dream ceases to exist, as well as all of his or her issues, problems, and frustrations that were part of the dream. Now in our so-called waking state in normal daily life, there is the possibility of shifting into another even more awakened state of awareness. Similarly when this "quantum" shift occurs, the personal self or identity dissolves just like our dream self did. It also was just a projection of subconscious drives, thoughts, and conditioning that appeared in our mind as the central organizing reference point of everyday experience. Likewise, just as when we awoke from our dream at night, all of our problems vanish instantly and remain so as long as the higher awake state of consciousness continues uninterrupted. By practicing being the objective observer to the events that arise continuously in consciousness, a new dynamic regarding the identification with this mind-generated sense of self occurs. Over time, there is a new feature to the flow of ordinary consciousness: the solidity of the self-projection diminishes. The sense of self is no longer quite so convincing nor are its problems so compelling and serious. It is not that the imagined self is progressing through stages of improvement, but it is more of a total dissolution of the imagined self. This dissolution of the imaginary self reveals the true nature of our beingness within, the actual source of our intrinsic deep peace, joy, and unconditional love. The true nature of our beingness *is this undefined and objective observing that has no name, identity, or history.* It is always present within all experience.

> Ego could be defined as whatever covers up basic goodness. From an experiential point of view, what is ego covering up? It's covering up our experience of just being here, just fully being where we are, so that we can relate with the immediacy of our experience. Egolessness is a state of mind that has complete confidence in the

sacredness of the world. It is unconditional well-being, unconditional joy that includes all the different qualities of our experience. (Tibetan Buddhist teacher Pema Chodron)

We discovered in the previous chapter there are the two essential aspects of the mind: thoughts and the awareness that is experiencing them. The awareness that is experiencing our thoughts and feelings remains unaffected from *all* childhood and later-in-life negative conditioning. This is like a mirror being unaffected by whatever reflections appear on it. However, for any benefit to be realized from this understanding of the mind, you must clearly recognize this unconditioned nature of the mind, our observing awareness. Too often the intensity of the mind's projections inhibit or block our being able to be in the objective role of just *being an observer*, like a spectator to our mind's activities. This takes work and effort in the initial stages of simply being an observer to the mind's activities. There is tremendous habitual momentum established that allows no room for self-reflection and detached observation of the mental events. We always get caught up in the mental stories and dramas that our minds weave.

In many ways, our daily state of mind is more akin to a trance than consciously aware living. That's because the aspect of our mind that projects our dreams while sleeping is also busy when we're awake projecting endless mental scenarios that oscillate between hope and fear. A good example is our sense of self. When dreaming we have a role and identity in whatever the scenario happens to be. We are not consciously creating this dream identity; it just arises from the subconscious. But it seems like who we really are in the dream. The emotional states and thoughts we experience in the dream are not questioned regarding their appropriateness and validity. When we awake, that dream identity vanishes, but we fail to notice that the mind is still projecting our sense of self and self-image. We don't even question the appropriateness of our emotional states, thoughts, or sense of self while awake. It is easy to see why many spiritual masters of different religious traditions have considered that mankind is asleep even while awake. This results in much of life's unnecessary suffering. We become lost in our stories, which are often based on conditioned responses and imagination, not the clarity of being vividly and alertly present to the current moment. There's a huge difference between the two. We aspire to the latter as we wake up from the former.

It's critical to discern between knowing who we actually are, as opposed to believing a story about who we *think* we are. In a dream we may suffer in many ways due to the drama in the story line. The one who suffers is our sense of "me" in the dream. If we only knew the entire story line was just an imaginary mental show, it would not be possible to suffer due to the dream's contents. A primary aspect that is necessary in order to suffer within the dream is to believe that the person you think you are in the dream is real. The dreaming mind creates not only the scenery and people in the dream but also a sense of personal subjectivity. There is no real person or self there, as the self is just a projection of the mind. Likewise the person you think you are in waking life is also a projection of mind and is not real, no more than Santa Claus or the Easter Bunny. Both of these fictional characters take on great life in the minds of children. But no matter how deeply and sincerely a child believes in Santa Claus, it will never make this fictional character real. Even so, the child can be motivated to act in certain ways by belief in this fiction. For example, the child can try to be better behaved or more obedient to "get presents from Santa."

Likewise notice all the behaviors we engage in because of our sense of self-identity that dictates an endless list of *shoulds, musts, should-nots,* and *must-nots.* As previously mentioned, we are always in one stage or another of acting out our polarized dramas, which swing between the aspirations of hope and the anticipations of fear. Do we ever really wake up from the dream of compulsive worry? Who is this that is always in the role of being a worrier? Remember, this troubled or suffering self is an add-on; it didn't come with the original hardware and software. We bought into it when we were really too young to know better. Now we know better. Or do we? We must remember that all of our psychological and emotional suffering comes from this belief in an imagined self-identity. How do we wake up from the waking dream of false self-identity based on conditioning? For starters, let's look a bit deeper into the nature of this self-illusion.

Just as we observed our thoughts in the second chapter, we now need to observe our sense of self as it arises in our minds. It's not different from any other thought, yet it seems much more intimate, doesn't it? By sitting quietly in an undisturbed environment, notice your sense of self. It's your sense of "me-ness." By remembering a time you were embarrassed or ridiculed publicly, you can get a profoundly clear sense of ego or self. When someone has spoken poorly of you, you might have thought, "How could they talk to *me* that way! The nerve of them!" Play around with this a bit until you get the self-conscious sense of personal *me-ness*. Now having done that, immediately observe this sense of self. Where does it seem to be in your body? Does it have a shape or color? Does it have substance? Is it different from any other thought? Is it just a thought? Is it just the *I* thought? Is there a sensation of *I am*? Who owns that sensation? What is that sensation?

When you were a baby there was a time when you had not developed this sense of me. What was that state of mind like? Imagine for a moment what that would feel like? There would be no inner sensation and self-definition of *I am*. In contrast, today you have a complete story of who you think you are. What would it feel like to be without your story of "me"?

All of our stress and suffering is based on this *me* story. Associated with that sense of self is also the sense of "mine."

The things and relationships that we consider as possessions cannot exist without first having a sense of personal selfhood as the owner. A large part of our worrying and stress is about our possessions, both material and relational. If suddenly we were free of the imagined sense of *me*, our possessions would be immediately liberated into being what they have always been—simply un-owned energies of the universe. If we examine our stressful thoughts regarding our possessions as well as our sense of self, we realize there is nothing of substance to our thoughts as thoughts. A thought is just a mental energy message that appears and disappears from time to time. This is also true of our sense of self. The problem is that we focus on the message and create an entire story from an initial brief flash of thought. If instead we looked at the thought as a mental energy event, not getting wrapped up in the content of its message, we experience an entirely different perspective. For example, if for two minutes we just counted the thoughts that passed through our consciousness, as opposed to getting involved in their messages, we would discover a much more open and relaxed state of mind. By practicing this simple exercise we can develop the ability to remain free of the trance-like condition in which we so often find ourselves throughout the day.

We need to develop this open state of mind to effectively notice the arising and continuing presence of the *me* thought. We discover that the *me* thought lies at the center of our psychological and emotional experiences from moment to moment. It's all about *me* and my story. The entire personal story revolves around *me*. Because of this we have a sense of being a separate individual living in a world of separate people as "others" existing "out there." This fundamental bifurcation of life experience into separate subjects and objects creates a general sense of existential alienation from the wholeness of life. We often feel alone and apart even though we may be living in a rich social context of family and friends. This is due to a personal story that revolves around the imagined notion of being a separate *me*. Over time this illusion becomes a default style of how we relate to ourselves and our world of experience. We may isolate ourselves further and further psychologically, eventually leading to states of depression and suicide. However, when we feel connected as a meaningful part of the whole, we flourish within our emotional lives.

In primitive societies the strong cultural reinforcement of life being an interconnected web of natural and ecological relationships is directly related to an inverse presence of psychological and emotional states of imbalance. Individuals consider themselves as integral parts of a cosmic wholeness with little concept of separate individuality. This holistic view of life permeates into social and ecological behaviors that further enhance the survival potential and well-being of the entire society. In our *me*-based Western culture we observe the insidious effects of this bifurcation between *me* and separate-from-me worlds. Ecological disasters abound across the planet, including global warming, deforestation, the rapid extinction of various species, air and water pollution, and the wasteful depletion of natural resources. I believe these social and planetary issues stem directly from the way our current culture defines who and what we are as individuals. This definition of self is then promoted and reinforced by parents to their children.

Our entire society is *me* driven, as represented in advertising that floods our consciousness daily. The message that you need to consume endless products is reinforced on many levels, and if you don't consume the right products you will somehow not be in the best social and personal position. So you need a bigger car, a better house, stylish clothing and accoutrements, plastic surgery, Botox, success seminars, and more, all in the name of enhancing *me*. At the same time, along with the rise and establishment of today's *me* culture, we have a similar increase in mental illness, suicide, crime, family structure breakdown, environmental neglect and abuse, and a generation of young people who have no real sense of connection with their natural world other than through the Internet, computer games, and social-media networking.

So there is great benefit to be had from breaking the *me* fixation, both personally and socially. The first step is to observe this sense of *me* as it arises in our consciousness. Throughout any given day, we are confronted with multiple opportunities to offer something beneficial, courteous, or kind that we often pass on. We fail to do the more self-less or ego-less thing because we are just caught up in the momentum and trance of "it's all about me." Here we have an opportunity to see our imagined sense of self at work. *Noticing this self-centeredness as it arises in our consciousness; is the practice.* Notice how the storyline of *me* is relentless in dictating our thoughts and behaviors throughout the day. It is also relentless in being a source of constant worry regarding its standing or position in social life scenarios.

But also from time to time notice that quality of aware observing that perceives this sense of me as it arises in consciousness. That observing awareness is the aspect of our consciousness that needs to be at the forefront of our cognitive life, not our sense of *me* and its conditioned reflexes. When we reside in our authentic sense of undefined being as this observing awareness, we are free to be everything, in the sense of a panoramic inclusivity. Our sense of self is no longer isolated from its world of experience; on the contrary, the mind can no longer find a line of demarcation separating it from its perceptions and relationships. Herein we have a possible method of return to a sense of wholeness and integration with our world. It is not that as an open awareness, we are not already integrated fully with our world; rather it becomes a noticed reality, as it has always been. It's only our thinking mind as opposed to our open awareness that imagines separation.

To further clarify, this simple open awareness is our default condition of noticing and knowing experiences as they arise, whether as thoughts, emotions, feelings, or sensory perceptions.

Observing awareness is present before the mind has time to think about the perceived experience. For example, if we hear a church bell ringing, at first it is just a pure sound occurring to our sensory system. In the next moment, the mind "kicks in" and identifies the sound as a church bell, along with any other associative thoughts. But then this simple awareness continues its ceaseless noticing of those very thoughts about the sound. Recognizing this default quality of changeless awareness in conscious experience is the heart of our method. This bright and vivid unconditioned awareness is our basic sanity. From engaging in this simple practice we initiate our own healing in terms of personal, social, and planetary health. Learning to live in unconditioned basic sanity develops insight into our true nature. Enlightenment is an illumination that reveals our observing awareness to be the Light and Life within everything. You will discover, without a doubt, that you are that unceasing Light of Awareness.

Question: But isn't our sense of ego as a *me* necessary in daily life? Is it practical to try to live an ego-less life considering the demands that our busy lives place on us?

Answer: Actually, because of the demands and stress that we continuously experience, it is far better to be awake and fully aware within the moment as opposed to being caught up in the imaginary world of me and my issues. In high-performance sports, it is well known that ultimate success can only be had when one is fully immersed in the now, devoid of any self-consciousness. This is sometimes referred to as "being in the zone" or "flow." How many times in life, whether at work or otherwise, have you been so engaged in a task that you lost all sense of time and personal self-consciousness? You notice the time and can't believe that two hours just disappeared. Without a cognitively present sense of self, you don't notice time. Along with that lack of self-consciousness, our personal problems and psychological issues are also nowhere to be found. So it would seem that operating in a mode of total involvement in our life's activities to the point of losing our selves in our task would enhance our performance and improve our mood. Instead of being focused in our thoughts *about* our activities, we focus our five senses and bodily actions directly with the environment and its physical components.

Our senses work well without the presence of thinking or self-consciousness but in harmony with an intuitive flow of intention that arises creatively in the moment. It is possible to simply relax into the observing presence of the five senses. You see, hear, taste, smell, and feel without self-consciously evaluating the perceptual experience. That's being in the now. In that fully present state, a type of intuitive knowingness guides one's actions in a flawless flow that is effortlessly integrated with one's world. Self-consciousness is a cognitive event where the *me* thought is in the mental mix regarding an activity. It's a subtle double-take in which you are in the event and looking in a mirror at yourself at the same time. This can be so strong that actors suffer from what is called stage fright. There is an overriding concern about how one's performance will be perceived. Of course this type of hindrance is not limited to actors; it occurs in all our lives from time to time. For me, I experience it in traffic when I notice a police car directly behind me. I lose my sense of carefree and relaxed driving and become absorbed in the thought of how my driving is being perceived. This is self-consciousness at work. What's interesting is that when we are in this self-conscious state we are more likely to make mistakes! That's the message: the less self-conscious we are, the better we do everything. The less self-conscious we are, the less we suffer. This is because it is only by reflecting on ourselves that we suffer. The less self-conscious we are, the more we fully participate in relationships and life in general. Self-consciousness is self-centeredness in slightly different garb. The less self-conscious we are, the more we can feel love and joy. So yes, learning to function in life free of the dictates of our conditioned imaginary self is realistic and life-enhancing.

Here's a progressive chart of self-conscious states:

Unconsciously self-conscious: Not aware of one's compulsive self-referencing. Consciousness fully identified as the conditioned sense of self.

Consciously self-conscious: Conscious of one's constant self-referencing. Observing with a sense of being a personal observer.

Absence of self-consciousness: Consciousness without self-referencing.

Naked Awareness. Observing without an observer. Doing without a doer.

Life just flows as a seamless stream of happenings not owned by anyone.

Question: What defines who the person actually is? It seems we have conscious and subconscious definitions that when added together comprise one's sense of identity. Who is the real me?

Answer: At an early age, we have no sense of identity. Then through social interaction, we begin to develop a sense of self based on conditioning and our inner reactions to that conditioning. However, we cannot deny that the organism has its own program that defines who we are on the most basic level. The DNA instructs the organism to survive and reproduce. It also drives the organism to control a certain amount of space in its immediate vicinity both for self-protection and for a space for offspring to be raised safely. These natural survival urges often find themselves in conflict with social, cultural, and religious codes of acceptable behavior. So the ego is often caught between subconscious urges and restraints imposed by cultural norms. You just can't do whatever the organic urges request without social consequences. As a result, the self seems to become split between two driving forces.

This produces inner conflict and anxiety. We also develop somewhere in early childhood, an "inner parent" that tells us what is right and what is wrong behavior. This inner parent is often referred to as the superego. Its job is to make sure you comply with social and familial codes of conduct to prevent you from being ostracized by the family or group. The organism associates expulsion and ostracization as hazardous to survival.

In our early primate evolution, monkeys found great survival benefit by remaining closely associated in tight groups. If a member was expelled from the group, the likelihood of long-term survival was greatly reduced. As a result, we have a powerful built-in mechanism that attempts to prevent us from being ostracized. It appears in the form of what we call our conscience. Even when a Nazi was not being a "good Nazi" according to the Nazi code of conduct, his conscience made him feel inner shame and guilt for deviating from the group mores. Unless he had a different group to join with greater or equivalent survival potential, he would feel uncomfortable about the potential of being ostracized. We can see by this example alone that our conditioned mind's sense of conscience is simply based on that conditioning and not some inner guide that is directing our behavior by some deeply imbedded sense of correct action or virtue. Of course, we also have a spiritually intuitive sense of basic goodness that is buried beneath all the social conditioning. All of this contributes to this basic split in personal identity. Am I my natural urges? Or am I my socially approved identity? Or am I something beyond defined identity altogether? Often this type of inner conflict, even though not clearly recognized as such, drains mental and emotional energy as the mind attempts to juggle opposing impulses. The effects can be chronic stress and anxiety.

But then let's step back and take a more panoramic view. Are you really any of those impulses or conceptualized identities? They do exist in the mind along with all of those pro-survival dynamics without doubt. But what is experiencing this inner complexity of tendencies, urges, and restraint? By simply observing these phenomena as they arise, without engaging them in any way, you discover that this naked observing awareness is in fact not defined by any of it. Herein is the discovery of true identity: that identity that can't be defined in any way beyond being this pure "observingness," within which we find the absence of any and all inner conflict. This is the discovery of a true and lasting peace of mind.

Question: Before a person can transcend this imaginary self, doesn't one first have to have a healthy and balanced sense of self?

Answer: In a sense this is true. But we are not actually transcending the imaginary self; we are learning to see through it as it becomes more and more transparent. However, if a person is severely neurotic or psychotic, the mind is too agitated by subconscious dynamics to recognize this healthy quality of aware being that lies within all states of consciousness. The witnessing awareness that notices our thoughts, emotions, sense of self, and perceptions is an unchanging mirror-like consciousness. It merely reflects what arises and appears in experience. The less reflection occurs in terms of mental events, the more likely the mirror will experience its own pure and unchanging clarity. The more powerful that the mental projection of a sense of *me* is, the mirror's own intrinsic clarity is less noticed. So it may be necessary at first to reduce the volume and intensity of the reflections before introducing the observing nature of the mirror itself. However, the best means of reducing the reflections, i.e., thoughts, stories, and negative emotional states, is by being a witness to mental events as they arise, thus creating some psychological space between the thoughts and the observing awareness.

Ultimately we need to realize that the imagined self does not exist. That sense of self is just a label and a sensation that your mind is creating in reference to your body and experience. It's like when in a darkened room you see a rope on the floor. The mind thinks it's a snake and the thought "snake" appears. Next adrenalin is released. The mind has applied the label "snake" to the rope. There is no snake yet the entire body and mind react as though there is. Likewise, the mind creates the notion of a self, an "I," in regard to the body and mind, just like the label "snake" was applied to the rope. But if we really examine this *I* thought and sensation closely, we won't find anything concrete that corresponds to this self idea as being real.

> It is important to remember always that the principle of egolessness does not mean that there was an ego in the first place...On the contrary, it means there was never any ego at all to begin with. To realize this is called "egolessness." (Sogyal Rinpoche, Tibetan Buddhist teacher)

We experience a 3-D image of what the mind thinks is "out there." It's a picture in our head. The eyes can't see any better than your toes. Eyes are passive receivers of light photons. They don't see anything. All those electro-chemical signals are figured out in the brain where a 3-D image is constructed along with a *viewer* of it. That "viewer of it" is also the mind's projection of an implied self at the center of experience. Without the mind creating that sense of a centralized self, there would be no sense of there being a self that is having experiences. There would just be experiences happening to no one, yet the vivid knowing of all experience would be sheer delight as there would be direct perceptual experience without any filters. This would be the same as when we were young children.

Question: If there is no personal self as we imagine, who owns our thoughts and memories? What happens to the notion of ownership?

Answer: That is exactly what we begin to discover. There is no owner of our thoughts and memories. They just happen. Who owns the rain or the clouds in the sky? The whole notion of own-ership is the mind's creative effort of connecting this imaginary *I* with several of the mind's perceptions and activities. This is quite natural as the *I* is intimately engaged with all thoughts and mem-ories. They all refer to this *I* in one way or another.

Question: Are there any easy and practical means to discover this aspect of there being "no self"?

Answer: David Bohm makes a great point in his book *Wholeness and the Implicate Order*. When we listen to music, he writes, the enjoyment we feel for the whole piece comes about through the immediacy of one note following another. If we slow the time down to the point where several minutes pass between each note, we would have no sense of the music. We could not sense the piece's direction or rhythm, and we would not have the same emotional response as if played at normal speed. The over-all effect of the music would be lost and escape our consciousness.

What if we applied that to meditation or just observing our thought stream? By sitting in open presence and just observing what arises without comment, without following thoughts into their alluring stories, the mind would eventually slow down. The sense of self, which is sustained by the constant rapidity of thought, becomes lost to experience. The sense of self is just a continuous series of thoughts and sensations associated and cen-tered around the *me* thought. Without the continuity of thought, we would lose the tune and meaning of the *self* experience. It has to be sustained by the constant and unceasing rapidity of thought that creates and maintains the illusion of there being a *me*.

Just like when you leave a muddy and murky puddle of water to settle, the water becomes clear as the muck settles to the bottom. The mind is the same. When we leave it undisturbed, thoughts slow down and the stories and structures of the mind collapse, including the illusion of there being a *me*. The longer you sit in stillness the better, until the *me* can no longer be discerned. Then you will be whistling a completely new tune.

Question: You say, "Without a doubt, you are that unceasing Light of Awareness." I have doubts. How can I come to know that I am that Light?

Answer: That is the purpose of this book: to provide instructions for that realization. The priority is to recognize the awareness that knows your thoughts, feelings, perceptions, and all experience. Notice how your awareness remains unchanging, but what it observes is in constant change. The scenery is always new, but the observingness is always the same. The more you are simply attentive to your perceptions without adding mental content regarding them, the more familiar you become with this naked perceiving or observing. Sometimes when sitting, just notice your surroundings without judgment or mental commentary.

Do the same when taking a walk, particularly in natural surroundings, and just silently observe. From time to time, notice this quality within your consciousness of thought-free observing. As you gain a subtle ability to discern your own observing awareness, it may become obvious that you are like a sphere of aware, clear light that is looking out your eyes. You *are* that sphere of clear light that is aware and perceiving. You seem to be centered in your skull looking out your eyes and listening through your ears. As your mind becomes more clear and silent, the fact of being an aware presence becomes apparent. That which is looking out your eyes at these words is that changeless aware presence. *Look back at that which is looking.* As your consciousness and attention become ever more settled in this condition of naked observance, insights into the nature of your awareness arise spontaneously. This is the beginning of the Light manifesting in consciousness, the Clear Light of Awareness, your true nature.

Chapter Four

The Nature of Awareness

Contemplative traditions such as Zen, Tibetan Buddhism, Yoga, and Taoism place a great emphasis on realizing the nature of our own awareness. Awareness is the only sentient or conscious element within thoughts, feelings, and perceptions. As the mind becomes calm and clear through meditation, or by whatever means, natural awareness becomes more obvious. The full understanding of this observing awareness is revealed in enlightenment. It is our true identity, a spiritual beingness that is not conditioned by experience in any way. Nothing can improve it and nothing can damage or diminish it. It's conscious, aware, and responsive. It does not require thoughts or knowledge in order to know. It knows by direct perception in "now-ness." It has amazing intuitive abilities that allow it to feel out a situation. It also has the capacity to exhibit phenomena such as telepathy and clairvoyance. It is not dependent on the body for its existence, yet it enters this dimension of material experience through a process of embodiment.

When the physical body ceases to function, your observing awareness, like a transparent, crystal sphere of clear light consciousness, separates from the body. The most important thing to realize is that this borderless sphere of pure awareness is who and what you are timelessly. Many people have had near-death experiences or conscious "out-of-body" experiences. These reports come from all cultures and describe a very similar theme and experience. I had such an experience in 1970 while living in Copenhagen. It changed my sense of self and self-identity permanently. I changed from being an agnostic to being a "believer" in a spiritual dimension of which we all are a part.

While living in Copenhagen, one day in 1970 I had just finished a meditation session and was walking back to my office in the same building where I worked. It was midday and most people were out to lunch. I was in a very relaxed state and was clear minded as I walked down the hallway to my office. Between the hallway and my office was a large reception area. As I began walking across the reception area, I suddenly noticed that my consciousness had moved out of my body in a full out-of-body experience. I had never experienced anything like that before. It was as though I was a sphere of knowing awareness floating across the room. I could see everything clearly and with a 360-degree periphery from my perspective, outside of the body. It seemed as though I was a bodiless ghost. I could see above me, below me, behind me, and in front all at the same time. I was approximately fifteen feet in front of my body as it continued to walk toward my office on the far side of the reception area. As I was floating toward my office, I suddenly felt as though I was in a metallic cage, looking through the bars as though I was in a jail cell. I could feel the temperature of the metal and sensed something like a metallic taste, even though I was without a mouth. I was confused and suddenly didn't know where I was. In a moment of orienting myself, I noticed that I had floated over the reception desk. It had three stacked metallic mesh in-baskets for holding mail. I had floated into the middle of the in-baskets and perceived their metallic substance. It was an amazing experience to feel something so directly and without a body.

I noticed my body was behind me and still walking in the direction of my office. Spontaneously I floated back into my head and was looking out of my body's eyes again. I opened the door to my office and walked in. I bent over to set my briefcase on the floor. As my body stood up, my consciousness stayed at the level of my waist or a little lower by my briefcase. I sensed this giant form lurching over me from above. As I oriented my perception upward, I noticed that it was my own body. I was out of my body again. I slowly floated back into my head and sat down at my desk. I remained in my body for the rest of the day. But the most amazing aspect was the fact that I now had total certainty that I, as conscious awareness, was not my body. It was as though my body was an automobile that I simply stepped out of for a few moments. This is the point where I came to know that I was not a physical body, but that I was indeed a spiritual being not subject to death. It seemed that I was a ball or sphere of clear, transparent awareness or consciousness, without any mass, solidity, or border. I was complete with my mind and sense of being myself but bodiless.

I later discovered there are specific practices in Tibetan Buddhism that discuss what they call the transference of consciousness teachings known as pho-wa in Tibetan. Here one trains on being able to consciously leave one's body in preparation for the eventual moment of death. Also in Taoism, one of the results of Taoist practice is that the sphere of conscious awareness, called the *shen*, or spirit, is able to leave the body and visit various realms and places in the universe while awake and fully conscious. I learned later that it's not so important to have an out-of-body experience, but it's more important to understand that consciousness or awareness is completely empty of any material components, like space, but vividly aware and independent of the body. It is this same consciousness or awareness that we discussed earlier—the awareness that experiences our thoughts and perceptions.

That out-of-body occurrence in Denmark was a strong motivating force that energized my deeper search into understanding my identity within a spiritual context. However, I was not able to resolve the issue of identity simply by that out-of-body experience. There still was a sense of individual existence apart from others and separate from the world in which I existed. However, I did have a deeper, more holistic intuition regarding the nature of reality. It became more apparent that our sense of separateness may continue beyond the death of the body or when out of the body. Realizing Oneness was something else again. In many spiritual traditions, it is considered that we have a mental body as well as a physical body and that when the physical body dies, consciousness continues in a mental body. This mental body is an energy form consisting of the most subtle energies of our life force, called *chi* or *prana* in Chinese or Indian systems of spiritual practice, respectively. In the West we associate this subtle mental body with that of the form of a ghost. Once we see our identification with the physical body as a misperception in our mind's assumptions, we recognize ourselves to be an aware consciousness that is independent of the body and its processes. That being said, it still doesn't change our sense of separation from the Whole. We have only attained the status of being something like a ghost floating around in space, bodiless. That certainly resolves our fear of death as being some sort of ultimate state of permanent extinction, but it doesn't qualify as what I would call enlightenment.

All of the traditions speak of enlightenment in terms of being a realization of "oneness" with the totality of life and the universe. Enlightenment is accompanied by a sense of peace, joy, and love for all beings. I couldn't say that this was my experience at that time, but it certainly was blissful and liberating in many ways. I remember a time after this out-of-body experience when I was living in Colorado. My girlfriend picked me up from the airport in Colorado Springs, and we were driving to my house in the foothills of the Rocky Mountains. As we came up the last section of road, I looked out the window and noticed the pine trees that lined the side of the road. My attention focused on one particular pine tree and its dark brown bark. For a moment it seemed that I felt the texture of the bark with my eyes and that my space of awareness expanded to include the tree. In that brief moment I could feel the tree's life force as the sun's warmth on the upper branches drew the sap upward from the roots. It felt as though the sap was passing through me. I felt as though I was that tree in that brief moment.

It wasn't imagination, it was an extrasensory experience. The tree seemed to have a type of consciousness that permeated all of organic life. This was clearly an experience of being one with nature as a whole. Many poets have expressed such experiences quite convincingly. This experience seemed intimately connected with my out-of-body experience of earlier years but was more centered on the being inseparable from phenomena as a whole. In the earlier "out of body" experience I did have the ability to "feel" textures and temperature as I did with the metallic in-baskets as I described. I learned later that these spiritual perceptions extended into the field of consciousness, being experienced as telepathy, clairvoyance, and synchronicity. I will share much more on this in later chapters that hopefully will offer greater insight into our spiritual capacities and how they unfold organically.

Stanislav Grof, psychiatrist and founder of transpersonal psychology, shared a similar story. One of his clients experienced a meditative type state he called transpersonal consciousness. *Transpersonal* refers to an experience beyond our localized self. It reveals wholeness and a depth of organic interconnectivity with everything we know. Having just read this account for the first time yesterday, I had to include it here because of its amazing similarity to my experience described above.

> I would have never considered seriously the possibility that there could be anything like plant consciousness. I have read some accounts of experiments pointing to the "secret life of plants" and claims that consciousness of

the gardener can influence the harvest. I always considered such stuff to be unsubstantiated and flaky New Age lore. But here I was, completely transformed into a giant Sequoia tree and it was absolutely clear to me that what I was experiencing actually occurs in nature, that I was now discovering dimensions of the cosmos that are usually hidden to our senses and intellects. The most superficial level of my experience seemed to be very physical and involved things that Western scientists have described, only seen from an entirely new angle—as consciousness processes guided by cosmic intelligence, rather than mechanical happenings in organic or unconscious matter. My body actually had the shape of the Sequoia tree, it *was* the Sequoia. I could feel the circulation of sap through an intricate system of capillaries under my bark. My consciousness followed the flow to the finest branches and needles and witnessed the mystery of communion of life with the sun—the photosynthesis. My awareness reached all the way into the root system. Even the exchange of water and nourishment from the earth was not a mechanical but a conscious, intelligent process.

However, the experience had deeper levels that were mythical and mystical, and these dimensions were intertwined with the physical aspects of Nature. Thus, photosynthesis was not just an amazing alchemical process, it was also direct contact with God, who was manifest through the rays of the sun.

The deepest level of the experience was purely spiritual. The consciousness of the Sequoia was a state of profound meditation. I felt amazing tranquility and serenity, as a quiet, unperturbed witness of the centuries. At one point my image of the Sequoia merged with that of a giant Buddha figure immersed in profound meditation, while the folly of the world passed me by. I thought about the transversal cuts through giant tree trunks that I had seen in the Sequoia National Park. On the mandala made of nearly four thousand annual rings various distances close to the surface, carry markers such as "French Revolution" or "Columbus discovers America" and another halfway to the center marks the year of Christ's Crucifixion. All the commotion of the world history meant very little to a being who had reached this state of consciousness.

—*Stanislav Grof,*
The Holotopic Mind

Upon reading this I was truly shocked at how accurately it described the inner content of my own transpersonal encounter with nature as it occurred thirty-six years ago in Colorado. The difference between the two was that in my case, I was in sensory contact with an actual, living pine tree.

What I discovered in my out-of-body experience was the actuality of our subtle body, a spiritual energy complex that exists as the mind's vehicle when the body dies. This complex of conscious energies is what is called the soul in almost all religious traditions. Some religious traditions consider the goal of religious life and practice is to become one with God. In Eastern traditions that has been expressed most overtly in Hinduism, as the purpose of yoga. *Yoga* means "union," union of the personal soul or self with God, Brahman, or Self. Buddhism refers to this Self through a much less anthropomorphic term called Nirvana. At the end of Buddhist practice you realize that the localized self was an illusion, a projection of mind. You realize that your true nature is Nirvana, a self-less state of pure Beingness, and this Beingness manifests itself as an apparent localized self that doesn't know its own origin. This is similar to the identity you appear to occupy in a dream that doesn't recognize its own self-identity as being just a projection from a deeper source.

It is possible *to recognize our cognitive presence as being a pure, unconditioned awareness within our immediate consciousness at any time.* We just need to be oriented to our aware presence as being who we are. The problem is that our attention is focused on our thoughts, sense of self, perceptions, and imagination instead of noticing the ever-present ground of current awareness or consciousness. It *is* possible to be in full awareness of our own spiritual condition without faith or belief in such a condition.

If we focus our sense of localized-aware presence in the area of the eyes or just behind; when we look out through our eyes, it's like we are looking out a window into the space in front of us. We are a borderless sphere of transparent awareness that has a provisional locus slightly behind and above the eyes. We are transparent, clear, and empty of content. We are a field of transparent, vivid openness intersecting with the body at the brain near the eyes. We have no actual center, but we have an orientation associated with the eyes, like our being a transparent, aware crystal-clear sphere, just floating in the head.

Like the glass in a mirror, the reflections or phenomena appear in our clarity. At no time do any of the phenomena condition our clear and changeless seeing. Noticing your awareness right now while looking out your eyes, feel how you are this pure, space-like seeing. It can be difficult to discern whether you are in the head or if the head is in you. Notice your lack of substance as being just this *pure seeing* without borders. You are completely transparent but vividly present. Notice that your existence is this sphere of clear awareness, pure seeing. In other words, be aware of your awareness. Notice how, as awareness, you are always right here. Thoughts cannot block awareness; thoughts are just appearances in you as awareness. The *me* and the personality are just appearances in your empty aware seeing. You are always you, always right here, clear and empty, exquisite clarity and being.

In this moment, notice what is looking at these words. This *pure* looking has no name, identity, or history. It is your changeless Nature.

Using the mirror analogy again, consider the natural state of our beingness to be like a vast mirror. All phenomena appear in it as reflections. Our mental or cognitive experience is one of only seeing, feeling, or noticing the reflections. How can we see or know the mirror, our essential nature? It's just like when you stand in front of the mirror looking at your reflection. You normally see the reflections only. But if you have to clean the mirror, you shift your seeing so that you are able to see the clear glass of the mirror instead of the reflections. We can do something similar in meditation or by simply noticing our condition. We shift our attention from being absorbed in our thoughts and images to releasing and relaxing that attentive absorption, and by so doing we are able to notice the vividness of our always-present naked awareness. That is how you notice the mirror of awareness. Then as a practice, continue releasing, relaxing, and noticing our vivid awareness again and again. Remember to bring your attention and awareness to your eyes, and notice the transparent nature of this clear seeing. As the practice progresses, notice how the releasing and relaxing becomes spontaneous. The thoughts and images arise and release on their own. Eventually even the slight effort required for noticing the vivid awareness dissolves, revealing *vivid awareness* to be our true nature that spontaneously pervades every experience.

In any case, you shouldn't accept my or anyone's descriptions of what this awareness may or may not be like. Investigate and find out exactly what your true nature is. Look backward into your awareness as though its right behind your eyes, the place from which you are looking. It's a looking into your center of consciousness. You will notice absolutely nothing is there, just this awareness. And notice again as you look out your eyes that you are the one looking. That looking is pure awareness, the unchanging perceptual nature of pure being. It's there by default, and nothing is required to sustain it.

Over many years, I discovered methods that made it possible to enter an inner state of investigative inquiry regarding the nature of our awareness. We can examine our thoughts, our sense of self, and the awareness that is the observing within all of our experiences. If we ask, "Who or what is aware?" or, "Who or what is knowing this experience?" we may discover that we can't find any fixed entity present. We can only find an impersonal condition of aware knowing. If we answer, "*I* am the one who is aware," then we need to ask, "Who or what is aware of this *I* sensation."

We should notice as well, that when this *self* sensation arises it is accompanied by the labels *I* or *me*. That *I* is just a thought, like any other thought. That being the case, we can recognize that the *I* thought that defines our sense of identity is as transparent as any other thought. Our true nature is what this *I* thought is arising *within*. But we are never this label or what it implies. We should spend some time observing this *me* thought and come to discover it's transparency for ourselves. Being free of the belief in the validity of the *me* thought is itself freedom from personal suffering. It is only that imaginary thought of *I* that arises as a suffering *me* from the subconscious.

As we continue to investigate the nature of our awareness, eventually we will discover the presence of an undefined *knower* of experience. It has no name or preferences. It has no history or story. You can't pinpoint its exact location other than the area just behind the eyes. You can't discover any shape or form to it. You can't observe it because it is at the exact place from where you are observing. How much closer could you get to where you already are?

Coming to total realization is recognizing the nature of your own being as pure awareness. When we discover our awareness to be an impersonal consciousness that is simply present as being, we may recognize that this awareness is a universal consciousness, the Ground of Being. Some may call it the Mind of God, the Buddha Mind, or the Self. Going forward, when we refer to this impersonal aspect of awareness, we will differentiate it by capitalizing the first letter of Awareness. Realizing universal Awareness is as simple as noticing the immediate lucid presence that is reading these words and recognizes the thoughts that arise about them.

Notice that your awareness has no shape or form. It is empty like space but aware and observing through your eyes and other senses.

Notice any current uncomfortable condition such as a contracted ego state, thought, emotion, energy state, sensory experience, or feeling. Observe the condition. Notice the feeling in the body. Just observe the feeling. Notice your awareness that is observing the feeling. See if you can find some part of that feeling of which you are not aware.

Notice if your awareness is at a distance from the feeling or is in direct contact with it. How close is your awareness to the feeling? Where is the feeling in relationship to your awareness of it? Next notice the empty aware quality of your observingness. Notice how the feeling cannot be separated from your awareness of it. *Consider that the feeling is your awareness of it, like waves being inseparable from the ocean.*

If there is an uncomfortable feeling, notice how it seems that your mind tries to disown the feeling by creating a sense of separation from it to avoid the uncomfortable sensation. It can't avoid the feeling but it may, through resistance, try to suppress it or contract it into unconsciousness. We do this with all experience that the mind finds uncomfortable to experience. We do this with thoughts as well as perceptions and feelings. Suppressing or repressing experience is the source of the material in the Freudian unconscious. All items in the unconscious are due to suppressed emotional reactions and the associated negative concepts or beliefs. Through resistance and denial, memory traces are left, like seeds of encysted energy. These seeds can blossom fully or partially in the future when a similar internal or environmental stimulus triggers the repressed memory and its energy. By not resisting our internal and external experiences, we can avoid further development of this reservoir of repressed memories. And when these memories and emotional energies are "triggered" again, we should simply allow them to appear exactly as they do and observe them without judgment or resistance. We eventually develop a new way of relating with our world of experience, a way that is much more relaxed and liberating.

The polar opposite of awareness is unawareness. The more dense or contracted our mental energy becomes through resistance, the less open and flexible our intelligence becomes. The ego state is itself a contraction of the mind's energy through a centripetal or self-centering force that limits its perimeter of experience. The ego state or sense of personal selfhood exists in relation to the presence of the *I* thought. In ego-consciousness, the mind becomes introverted by its own self-referencing like an intrinsic narcissism. Our sense of self is an energy projection of the mind, like being a character in our dreams. In our dreams, we don't realize our individuality is simply a temporary projection of the mind. It's also the same while we are awake. But in this case, when it is experienced directly that our waking sense of self is simply a projection of the subconscious mind, our sense of self-identity is then known to be an illusion. This is the realization of *no self*. We function fine after this realization because the mind is no longer burdened with the complex actions of managing this illusory self. Awareness is now acting directly without the intermediary interference of an ego or conditioned self.

The recognition that all thoughts are actually modulations of the energy of Awareness is a primary insight. All of these thoughts arise in the mind and dissolve from moment to moment. Thought is a wave-like vibration of conscious energy with informational significance. Thoughts occur in awareness, like reflections in a mirror. The mind is itself the creative energy of awareness appearing in the energy forms of thought and imagination. This energy field of the mind surrounds this non-dimensional point of aware consciousness like an aura or, when contracted, like a cocoon. This is the subtle mental body. The subjective experience of self-consciousness is its own energy field centered around the *I* thought. In other words, when the sky is filled with clouds or the mind is filled with thoughts, we experience a cloudy day or a mentally absorbed moment. The sky has not been altered by the presence of the clouds, nor has awareness been altered by the presence of thoughts or mental content. But regarding the mind, the mental content is our experience in that moment. So Awareness doesn't change, only its contextual content does. *Recognizing this unchanging aspect of awareness is a significant break-through in terms of personal liberation.*

As mentioned earlier, the primary way the mind determines the content and quality of experience is through the power of attention. That is done by placing attention on whatever our desired focus happens to be. The two possibilities regarding the placement of our attention are: reside in the contents of the mind absorbed in thought, or reside as the naked awareness in which all thought content appears. Both dynamics run parallel along the same time line. The naked presence of perceiving awareness co-exists along with the content-filled mind. If not, then there would be no perception of experience. We can settle our attention within the open observing aspect of awareness, or we can be attentive to the mind's contents and activities. Freedom is found in this vividly empty space of observing awareness. There is no suffering or confusion possible in this condition, whereas all our problems and suffering come from being absorbed in the stories and day-dreams that make up the *contents* of our mind. It is important to note that the sense of self is the central pillar that sustains the mind's absorption in its content. All the stories in my mind are centered around me and how I assess my situations. That being the case we need to look once again into this sense of me that is the focus of the mind's attention.

Notice that your consciousness is aware and empty, yet it appears to take the form of being a subjective personal identity. This would be like a single cloud dominating the open sky, where the cloud is the *me* thought and the open sky is our awareness. We recognize that a cloud arises and disappears within the sky. So in a sense the cloud and the sky are really not so separate after all. As the cloud dissolves in the atmosphere, we are left with the emptiness of the sky. We could then say that the emptiness of the sky is also the emptiness inherent in the cloud. The form of the cloud is always provisional; it will return to its emptiness in oneness with the sky. Thoughts arise from the emptiness of the mind and resolve again into that emptiness. They never take on a separate existence independent from the awareness in which they appear. So we could say that thoughts are essentially empty of any inherently existing form as they vanish again and again, like clouds in the sky. However, to the mind, the stories told by these momentary thoughts take on a certain reality to the degree that the mind energizes them through paying attention to them. But just as the various forms that clouds may assume in the sky, the mind's stories, the forms of our thoughts, all dissolve into emptiness. If only we could recognize the complete emptiness of our mind's stories right from the beginning, so much suffering and worrying could be avoided. Well, it is possible to do just that.

The spacious emptiness of our observing mind and its appearances in terms of thoughts both exist in the same moment and at the same location, like reflections appearing in the glass of a mirror. The cognitive knowing of experience is a quality of the aware emptiness or aware space. Conceptual significance and energy intensity are the defining aspects of the form of thought. The empty awareness permeates the form of thought non-dualistically as water does a wave. Thought is a wave of awareness. Recognizing the empty awareness present within all mental phenomena experienced, such as a perception, feeling or thought, reveals the form to be empty awareness at root and so it releases and transforms back into its naked essence as awareness. This is the method of self-liberation. It's not that we have to "do" something to "self-liberate" thoughts; they automatically reveal their intrinsic impermanence moment to moment. We simply take the position of purely experiencing all perceived phenomena free of evaluation. Notice how your naked-aware perceiving is changeless whether thoughts, self-fixation, suffering, or pain arise. Its mode is oneness with everything. Its path is always leaving everything as-is. What effort is there in noticing things exactly in the way you experience them?

When *leaving everything as-is* fully matures, the mind and thinking dissolve into their transparent origin. Suddenly, an enlightening insight arises, an aspect of gnosis or non-conceptual mystical wisdom. It is only this gnosis that can transform the ignorance that exists within consciousness. Through this transformation, all phenomena within consciousness reveals their impermanent nature to be emptiness—the empty nature of awareness itself. This too is liberation and realization.

For example, when we observe a thought, it changes in the next moment. That exact thought experience may be replaced with something similar, but the original thought is permanently gone. This is also true when we observe a tree, for example. We never experience the tree per se, we only experience the impression made within consciousness by interaction with the five senses. We never experience the same tree twice; the perceptual experience of the tree is always a fresh impression through the senses. What we do experience is a brain-generated, colored image of what it imagines the tree looks like based on sensory input and similar past impressions. That 3-D image is made of the same stuff as thoughts and dreams. Therefore the impermanent empty nature of thought is the same impermanent empty nature of our experience of the "outside" world. We never experience an outside world, but only the processed sensory impressions that appear within our inner world. Further, current quantum physics tells us that what we call solid matter is not solid at all. Nothing is solid or enduring in any way. But our brain is always trying to make the world seem as solid as possible. A chair for instance is a seething mass of movement that is more empty space than energy. The unchanging chair as a fixed, solid object in space and time is an illusion created by the mind. Scientifically there is no doubt about this.

Unfortunately the mind's tendency to impose a quality of enduring solidity to objects also applies to its sense of self as being an enduring thing. We become fixed in our opinions about ourselves and our world of experience. This becomes extremely frustrating for the mind because eventually everything that the mind imagined to be fixed and enduring reveals itself to be impermanent and empty of any enduring solidity, including itself. Hence its fruitless efforts at trying to construct a sense of personal security around itself through acquisition of ever increasing amounts of money, power, and influence. This dynamic to maintain the solidity of self and its world is the root of human suffering. And this entirely unnecessary tragedy that only occurs in our minds, is due to not realizing the true nature of being as changeless Awareness.

The term *Buddha* means "the awoken one." From what did he awaken? He awoke from the dream projection of the mind and its imaginary self or ego. The dream is our mind's story, which is made up of thoughts, identities, imagination, and conditioning. All suffering exists only in this story. It is not that you are depressed, it is only your ego or false-self that is depressed. It is not that you are angry, it is only that your ego is angry, and so on. That means that it is only your ego that suffers. On the cessation of the dream of self and its story, suffering ceases and you recognize yourself to be undefined and unchanging Aware Being. Aware Being is never asleep. It's aware during sleep, dreaming, thinking, in life and in death. It's just not usually noticed. Aware Being knowing Itself is enlightenment. Our true nature has no preferences, goals, plans, or problems. It's not enmeshed in a story. It has no desires or thoughts. It never becomes confused. It has no sense of personal self. It has no sense of possessiveness. Yet it empowers all that is into apparent existence in total spontaneity. The only freedom to be found is in being fully awake to what you are.

Question: Could you explain in more detail how by realizing the emptiness of the perception, thought, or feeling, it will release back into the awareness from which it arose?

Answer: If during an experience of a thought or mental occurrence of any kind we notice the empty quality of our observing awareness that is perceiving the thought, the occurrence will diminish or dissolve. By doing this we are actually realizing the empty or transient nature of the occurrence.

The occurrence, remember, exists in our consciousness. The only objects that occur in consciousness are thoughts or mental perceptions because the mind or brain creates a 3-D representation from the "external" sensory input of which we then become "conscious." In other words, external objects never appear in our consciousness, only the mind's representation of them. For our purposes, we could consider all objects that appear in consciousness to be waves of awareness, as there is no separate substance that shows up in our mind other than consciousness itself appearing as the forms experienced. This is similar to saying that when we have a dream, all the things and people that appear in the dream are made of dream "stuff" or mental images. That means that everything we experience in consciousness is an aspect of consciousness itself and consciousness as awareness is fundamentally a clear emptiness. That means the essential nature of our thoughts, feelings, or perceptions are also empty, like the content of our dreams. When we wake up in the morning, we realize the absolute emptiness of our dream world. It never had solidity of any kind, but it seemed solid and real during the dream. It was just a projection of mind. Likewise, our mental experiences that arise in waking consciousness have no actual substance either. It is this recognition of the emptiness of our thoughts, mental events, and sense of self that liberates us from our dreamlike world of suffering and anxiety.

Question: What exactly is this state of oneness that you are describing?

Answer: When consciousness shifts into a higher mode of aware perception, the sense of self dissolves as a fixed point in space and time. We could borrow the concept of quantum physics in which light is a localized particle, a photon or a non-localized wave. It is the same with consciousness. We can seem as though we are individual souls as spheres of consciousness, or we can appear as non-localized consciousness, like an unlimited ocean of Awareness. When this dissolution of self-belief occurs, consciousness is beyond any borders or specific identification as being some "thing" or person. There is a Universal Intelligence that permeates all of existence without any limits. We are that Intelligence, and as such we are able to sense our boundless Presence as being within and as everything. It's an actual cognitive experience that arises at the moment the mind is free of all fixations, concepts, and sense of ego or personal selfhood.

In the meditative traditions, this state of non-localized being is experienced in what is called *samadhi*, which is a non-dualistic state of consciousness where the Oneness of Reality is directly known. For most contemplative traditions, this state occurs by perfecting the practice of meditation. In this meditation, the mind is encouraged to become perfectly still through concentration and breathing exercises. At some point the mind may come to perfect stillness, meaning all thoughts have stopped and the sense of being a separate self, which was just made up of thoughts, dissolves. If we do manage to still the mind, there remains an awareness that notices the stillness. That awareness is the same one that notices thoughts and perceptions. It is never in a dualistic condition in relationship to its experience. It has no personal sense of self. It doesn't think or imagine. Yet it is always the presence of our undefined, conscious awareness. However, there is a less well-known way of accomplishing samadhi without meditation practices and efforts to still the mind. By simply relaxing one's thinking mind into being a nonjudgmental observing presence, the mind naturally collapses into the stillness that is the essential nature of this observing awareness. At that point the energy of the mind is in the naked condition of attentive alertness, instead of active thought. By continuing in this naked perceiving, the awareness itself reveals its own inner dynamics and a natural state of non-dual samadhi is *revealed*, not created. This is the method that I am sharing in this book as the essential means to recognizing the already enlightened nature of mind that resides within and as the core of our existing consciousness.

From the out-of-body experience in Denmark, I knew that this witnessing consciousness was independent of the body and brain. I also perceived that it has no material substance, is clear and transparent, yet vividly alert and aware. And most importantly I realized this awareness to be the essential nature of my own existential presence. Through various methods it is possible to further realize the full potential and nature of our ever-present awareness. We also discover that we are not just passive witnesses of experience and life; we are part of an interpenetrating web of relationships that connect us all in otherwise unimaginable ways.

Question: You mentioned that our experiences of the "outer world" only occur in our brain or mind. But it seems we are seeing various events happening all around us all the time. Would you please expand a bit on this topic? And also, what then is the substance of our mind?

Answer: The perceptions of the five senses register as conscious experience in the brain. No one has ever experienced anything outside of their own conscious experience within their mind. The brain receives sensory impressions, processes the information, and creates a 3-D image that represents what it believes is "out there." It has to be that way because the eyes can't see anything. The eyes simply register the impact of photons on the cones in the retina. The brain then takes those impacts or stimulations and makes sense of them by representing them in a 3-D image or movie that our consciousness experiences. We call that inner 3-D mental experience "everyday life." Since our world is limited to our perceptions as processed through the five senses and that information only exists in our mind, we realize that all experience only occurs within our mind.

What is the substance of our mind? It is only thoughts and images, the same substance as our dreams. Since thoughts are essentially empty of any enduring reality, our world of experience is also lacking any enduring reality. From moment to moment, our world arises within our mind as perceived by our awareness and dissolves in the next moment. Each moment is fresh and complete, yet empty and devoid of all permanence. This is the ego's dilemma: how to enjoy the moment without having it dissolve in the next. It also senses that its own existence is doomed to the same fate, and this can create a sense of panic when first recognized. So the ego solution is to try to solidify experience as much as possible in hope that things may endure a bit longer, including itself. This of course is a futile effort and hence creates great suffering and frustration for the ego-self. The awareness observing all the mental drama of the ego is always fully present, but as though it is observing from the audience as the ego story is taking place front stage under the bright spotlight of the mind's focus of attention. By shifting the spotlight from the ego on stage to the observer in the audience, we find immediate liberation. We accomplish this by "looking back at what is looking out our eyes."

Chapter Five

Three Essential Approaches to Realization

There are essentially three approaches to realization within the frameworks or paradigms in which I have been taught. In practice, the most appropriate approach would be dictated by the capacity of the student. In the direct-awareness approach, also called immediate realization, there is no concept that there is something wrong with the student that needs fixing. The perspective of this teaching is taking the goal as the path. The goal is realizing the core aspect of consciousness that has always been perfect and has never needed improvement in the first place. We need to recognize that core aspect of consciousness as being our current perceiving awareness as it is. The path of practice is simply remaining in recognition of the existing naked awareness that we just recognized. It is the knowingness within all experience. It is the changeless perceiving within all changing phenomena whether as perceptions, sensations, feelings, emotions, or thoughts. This default observing awareness is always a non-evaluating observing. It is an observing without a defined observer. It is awareness without thoughts about the various experiences observed. The *thinking about* comes later when and if the conceptualizing mind becomes active.

For example, it is through opening our eyes that seeing just happens. No one is making seeing happen. The seeing is there by default. It's completely impersonal, meaning that it remains the same sensory function whether you have a personal sense of identity or not. The same applies when we hear a sound. We don't have to do something special to make hearing happen. This is true for all five senses as well. But most of us don't notice that we also have an impersonal, default quality of consciousness or awareness present at all times. It is that awareness that is registering input from the five senses and noticing all thoughts and mental phenomena as well. It is possible that someone could recognize this default, impersonal quality of observing awareness as being who and what they actually are, as opposed to the mind's believing in an imagined identity. This newly recognized observing awareness is timeless and changeless presence, our True Nature. It is this sudden shift of self-recognition that is aimed at through the methods of the direct-awareness approach, or immediate realization. It seems those who have immediate self-realization with this approach on their first exposure are much less burdened with psychological issues and intellectual grasping to begin with. They are more open and ripe for this type of skillful intervention. We could say these individuals are of the highest capacity.

The second approach is for the more average seeker. This approach directs the student to engage in gradual practices of meditation in order to bring the mind to some degree of stillness, calm peacefulness, and transparency. Most Zen today is taught through the gradual approach to realization. This approach requires periods of sitting meditation and a practice of mindfulness throughout one's daily activities. Mindfulness training is simply being mindful of what you're doing as your doing it. In other words, you are present to your actions, feelings, thoughts, and perceptions in immediate experience, as opposed to fumbling through your day in a mental fog or a state of trance-like daydreaming. Through many months of this type of training, you may come to a significant state of clarity, significant enough to warrant moving into the first category of approach mentioned above. Because your mind has been brought to a greater state of stillness and transparency, a more mature condition develops that could be called "ripeness." The student would then be "easy pickings" for a teacher of the *direct awareness* approach. In my experience, the bulk of seekers fit appropriately into this gradual-approach category, at least initially.

The third approach deals with yogic practices that work with the internal energies of the body along with meditation. These practices may include yogic meditation postures, clearing blockages within the inner subtle energy body and seeking to transform our ordinary state of mind into that of an enlightened higher consciousness. It doesn't matter what one's philosophical or religious beliefs are in this case, as they will all be dissolved along with ego-consciousness through the use of the energy practices. What remains is your original pristine awareness in the knowing of its own spiritual Beingness. Although this approach is the most strenuous, it is the most profound in its depth of realization. All doubts regarding your true spiritual identity are swept away.

As a teacher, I use all three approaches, often in combination based on the capacity of the student. The realization is ultimately the same in all three approaches, with slightly different nuances based on the differences within each student's constitution. Let's examine the three approaches in greater detail.

I like to refer to the immediate-realization approach as the direct-awareness approach because the entire modus operandi of the methods is geared around the internal dynamics of awareness itself. This approach is simply to recognize the existing perfect aspect of consciousness that is the awareness within the stream of experience in terms of thoughts and sensory perceptions. Then after authentic recognition has occurred, one simply rests as that changeless awareness allowing it to blossom fully as it transforms other states of mind naturally and organically into itself. No other agency is required. It is understood that we have within our own consciousness the full capacity to realize our own true nature without any knowledge or special transmission acquired from without. Let's now continue by acquiring a deeper understanding of the most basic concepts regarding the direct-awareness approach.

Most important is the understanding regarding the nature of mind and consciousness. We have two essential components within all conscious experience. One is our thinking, conceptualizing, and imagining mind; the other is the awareness that is conscious of all mental and perceptual events. The central pillar of this approach is this *observingness* or *knowing awareness* that is already within all experience. It is this knowing awareness that the teacher is attempting to point out to the student conclusively and beyond any doubt. The student actually recognizes himself or herself to be the unchanging, perfect knowing awareness. This knowing awareness is a very naked witnessing or perceiving awareness. It is free of the clothing of thought, has no sense of personal identity, or a personal story regarding its history. It is like our five senses: our eyes just see without any sense of being some defined "seer." Hearing is the same in that we just hear sounds without the capacity to hear being defined as a specific "listener." Likewise, our naked awareness is just the noticing or observing within the interior mental events as well as the "external" perceptual events of experience. We also notice that this observing occurs with no sense of a personal identity as the "observer." This would be like a newborn baby just observing its environment without any sense of it being a defined identity.

Immediately after an experiential sensory event, the mind begins labeling, judging, and otherwise categorizing the input as received. This is the same for all five senses. Initially the sensory input is nakedly seen or heard as is, as raw perception, the immediacy of awareness. However, a split second later the mind kicks in and begins to process the sensory input further. So in this way our awareness is just like our five senses. Awareness never processes the perceptions; it just experiences them as is. Also, just like the five senses being there by default regardless of the mind's activities, so too our awareness is a default presence. It turns out we are always aware, awareness is always switched on. It is even present when we dream, as it is the awareness that notices and empowers the dream and its contents.

In contrast to this unchanging awareness, we also have the activities of the mind that are always changing. It is this unchanging awareness that experiences and empowers all the mind's activities. It is the thinking mind that creates or conceptualizes a sense of personal identity. It is again unchanging awareness that experiences and empowers these thoughts about personal identity. The naked awareness has no concept of identity, hence it has no ego to remove or reduce.

At this point, the teacher may use the example of a mirror and its reflections. The mirror would be pointed out to be like the unchanging, perceiving awareness, and all the thoughts and mental activities would be like the reflections. At no time do the reflections condition the glass of the mirror. Reflections would be pointed out to include thoughts, identity, emotions, feelings, sensations, and sensory perceptions. It is possible that based on this explanation alone, the student may have a sudden insight recognizing his most essential true nature to *be the unchanging awareness within the mind as opposed to its contents*. If this insight hasn't arisen spontaneously on the student's mind-stream, the teacher would continue with various examples and explanations until the student's intrinsic awareness-wisdom arises suddenly in a moment of realization.

Once the initial realization of his or her true nature occurs, the student is instructed to just continue in that enlightened self-recognition that arises from moment to moment. The enlightened insight is actually arising in every moment of our experience. However, our attention goes to and becomes the mind's content and activities instead. So we are taught to relax vividly and alertly with no mental agenda or topic whatsoever, which then allows the always arising enlightened wisdom-insight to be recognized from moment to moment. Often, due to the mind's self-distraction instead of the wisdom-insight energy of the mind being experienced as "realization," the energy potential of wisdom-insight itself transforms into thoughts and imagination. That's why realization and ego-consciousness are mutually exclusive.

We then simply continue in this profound condition of realization without engaging further in the various elaborations of thought and conceptualization. The mind will kick in from time to time with introverting stories about "me" and "my issues," but those appearances will dissolve upon their arising as we continue in our actual condition. Eventually our thought processes become more and more transparent as our natural condition of awareness outshines the mind's activities.

In Zen there is the Sudden Enlightenment School. It is a unique tradition stemming from the sixth Patriarch of Zen in China, Huineng, from the seventh century. One of the key tenets of this tradition is the notion of "no mind" or the non-activation of the thinking process. It is considered that all of our troubles come from the thinking process and believing what thoughts tell us. In this case the goal is not for the student to suppress thoughts and thinking, but rather to recognize the ever-present awareness that is experiencing those mental events, from within those mental events and as inseparable from those mental events. In the context of Zen, that would be called recognizing one's intrinsic Buddha Mind or Self-Nature. In the moment of this recognition, the mind becomes still. In this stillness we find a window of opportunity to recognize that which is always present but not noticed during mental and conceptual engagement.

This sudden realization often reveals itself when some occurrence has triggered an immediate and complete insight into the nature of self and reality. Often it could be an interview with a Zen master in which the teacher saw the exact obstacle barring total realization in the mind of the student and brought attention to it suddenly and often obliquely.

In 1978 I visited Hong Kong and had hopes of finding a Zen teacher in China. I was looking for original teachings from the ancient school of "sudden enlightenment" of Huineng's lineage, the Sixth Patriarch of Zen or Chan, in China. *Chan* is the Chinese word for Zen. I was referred to an elderly gentleman who was the Chan master of three separate temple monasteries. His name was Yen Wai Shih, a disciple of the venerable master Hsu Yun, who was the holder of all five ancient lineages of Zen in China. Yen Wai Shih was eighty-four years old when I met him. His teacher, Hsu Yun, died in 1959 at age 119! One of the three temples was on the island of Lun Tao, and two were on mainland China, in Shatin, part of the New Territories. I met this teacher first in mainland China at one of his temples in Shatin. I spent the entire day with him, discussing everything about "sudden enlightenment" and how to attain it in the shortest time possible. It was from that discussion that I first experienced a true flash of enlightenment, called *satori* or *kensho* in Japanese, and *wu* in Chinese. I'll share a bit of the conversation and meeting:

From Hong Kong I took a ferry to mainland China and had to find my way to Shatin, the location of Yen Wai Shih's temples and monastery complex. He greeted me in the village, and we walked up into the lush foothills of Shatin. We saw several older villagers in a lower temple room busily chanting randomly and lighting incense sticks in great abundance; the fragrance was intoxicating. Thinking this was a Zen temple, I didn't understand what all this other stuff was about. Hoping not to offend my teacher or confess my ignorance prematurely, I took the risk to ask him what those people were doing. In response he said "God only knows," and we both had a good laugh! Now you have to remember the image this venerable eighty-four-year-old Zen master offered in his simple yet functional Zen monk's robe in contrast to his off-handed comment about his own disciples; it was so completely disarming! That was our first point of human contact—heart to heart.

We continued walking upward, the stairs continuing to ascend to higher and higher temple grounds and buildings. We finally came to a house where Yen Wai resided. I was introduced to his granddaughter and family. I was amazed at their sense of reverence for this elderly patriarch of the family. You could tell they knew he was more than just a nice and kindly grandfather, and that they intuitively knew his value to those fortunate enough to have contact with him. And now it was my turn to try to understand what they already knew.

We talked about many things concerning Buddhist teachings and how to understand true enlightenment. I told him that above all other things I wanted to understand and experience my Enlightened Nature firsthand. I shared with him many of my intellectual thoughts about the true meaning of practice and the enlightened state of mind. He was quite amazing in his command of English. He spoke with a deep bass tone and flawless British accent. In his earlier years he had studied and fallen in love with the writings of Shakespeare. He insisted Shakespeare was an enlightened being. More amazing was the fact that when I asked him about points of Zen teachings, he would often quote phrases from Shakespeare to make his points vividly clear! Can you imagine how this whole scene took place as if in some surrealistic space somewhere between ancient China and Medieval England? Truly unsettling.

We continued walking the grounds and eventually arrived at a monastery of his disciples, both men and women in different sections. Most of the Buddhist nuns were already well beyond middle-age. They were nothing less than wonderful in expressing warm greetings to both of us. They had something special to offer—a stew of freshly picked and stir-fried giant shiitake-like black mushrooms. To this day, I can't think of a meal I ever enjoyed more, so simple yet delicate in the array of subtle flavors, as though I was eating the essence of the entire mist enshrouded forest from which these mushrooms were gathered. I know also from observing the demeanor of these elderly women that each mushroom was savored at the picking as being a precious offering of the forest, yielding nutrition and *chi* (Chinese for "life force") to restore the vitality of all those servants of the Way.

We finally arrived at our destination, a residence that housed some of the senior monks and guests. We went upstairs to Yen Wai's study, where we were greeted with tea and biscuits. The tea was a bit strong for my tastes, but certainly set the sober mood. Now was my chance to ask more of my burning questions, the ones I was leading up to yet approaching obliquely so as not to expose my shallow knowledge all at once. Perhaps I had a fear that if I appeared as too much of a novice he might reserve the best of his enlightening morsels of wisdom for a later time, when I would have ripened more. Ripening more, for me, was just twisting longer in torment on the vine of my own unenlightenment, a state I already knew all too well. Hell, that was why I took all the trouble to come this far, wasn't it? Let's not fall now, I thought, clearly aware that I was free-climbing with no ropes or safety equipment on the face of a totally unpredictable mountain. It could be my final salvation if scaled adroitly or be my demise, at least in spirit. Who else could I visit and interview about the ultimate meaning of the Buddha's teaching? My short list of candidates was dwindling. After all, I was interested in the shortest path to enlightenment, the teachings of the Sudden School of Enlightenment of the Sixth Patriarch. These teachings were renowned as the source of instruction that brought the greatest flowering of Zen masters of all time! If not Yen Wai Shih, an actual master of this lineage, then who?

We sat drinking tea discussing the true meaning of Wu or enlightenment. *Wu* has a particular meaning in Chinese; it's a way of asking about one's Buddha Nature. From his precise and direct explanations, I thought I finally grasped the true essence of the teaching. Proud of my realization I asked him this question:

"So master, I understand the purpose of practice is to just simplify one's thinking completely. Isn't that it?"

I waited expecting his nod of approval and confirmation of my understanding. Instantly, like a master samurai drawing his *katana*, his sword, and striking a singular killing blow, he lurched toward me with the authority of a granite mountain.

"You have already made "It" hopelessly complex!!!" he exclaimed.

My mind went completely blank. BLANK, EMPTY....WU There it was....HA!!! We looked at each other, and his eyes locked on mine. There was no movement, and suddenly as though Mt. Fuji was erupting, we both exploded in laughter. I couldn't stop laughing. I stood up and danced around in hysterical laughing.

"I see...I see....yes," I said. "To simplify is to make it hopelessly complex!"

Ha, ha, ha.... laughing; we must have laughed for five minutes, at least! He smiled broadly, his eyes filled with mirth as we both recognized that his skillful and thoroughly spontaneous blow cut through to the marrow and transformed the space of my mind into Wu. That's how I came to know the Way, as taught by the Sudden Enlightenment School of the Sixth Patriarch of Chan, the illustrious and profoundly compassionate Huineng. At a later time, Master Yen Wai gave me permission to teach others according to this style of "sudden" Zen.

An ancient Zen story tells how one day, a monk disciple came upon his Zen teacher and asked:

"How master may I come to perceive my Buddha Nature?"

The master responded, "You cannot perceive your Buddha Nature because *that* which *perceives* is your Buddha Nature."

This type of approach to a sudden awakening of profound, enlightened insight is limited to Zen, two traditions within Tibetan Buddhism and Advaita Vedanta. One of the Tibetan traditions is called *Dzogchen*, pronounced as it looks. It is called the Great Perfection in English. Dzog means "perfection" and *chen* means "great" in Tibetan. The Great Perfection teachings discuss this primordial perfection that is our own naked awareness, the consciousness through which we experience whatever occurs in life, yet is itself unmodified in all experience. The Great Perfection method is one in which the teacher directly introduces the student to his own awareness through a descriptive "pointing out" that focuses the mind on its most essential nature directly and abruptly. If executed properly the student has at minimum a glimpse of the enlightened state. The student is then instructed to keep that insight alive by simply continuing to rest and relax in that newly exposed state of being, without engaging the mind in conceptualizing about what just "happened." An important instruction is *to remain completely relaxed at all times, yet vividly alert and empty of any mental topic or focus.* That is a hallmark of all Dzogchen teachings.

In Tibet, the Great Perfection teachings receive the highest respect from all four schools of Tibetan Buddhism. Until recently, the Great Perfection teachings were kept secret, and it was almost impossible for a Westerner to receive actual Great Perfection teachings from a Tibetan lama. But around forty years ago, the highest lamas decided to open the Great Perfection teachings to Westerners.

I have found the Great Perfection teachings to be the most powerful of all immediate-realization or direct-awareness approaches.

Here is an ancient quote from a fundamental Great Perfection Tantra, or scriptural text, called the "The Heaped Jewels." It completely summarizes the unique method of Dzogchen practice.

> When anyone rests in the natural state without concentration, understanding manifests in that individual's mind, without someone having to teach all the words by which the mind understands these meanings. As this understanding dawns in the mind, all that is non-manifest and all sensory appearances, which in themselves entail no concepts, are seen to be naturally pure. (From *Longchenpa's Precious Treasury*, Padma Publications.)

What does "resting in the natural state" mean? It is simply to be present to immediate now-ness, which is our naked presence of fundamental awareness—a pure observing and simple awareness of the moment without a program, topic, or agenda. This topic-free, judgment-free observing, fully alive and alert, is our natural state. Through the mind, we add on top of this foundational awareness a layer of thought, a sense of self as the observer, and an assessment of what we observe. These added layers can be considered clothing on consciousness. What we want instead is to simply rest as *naked* awareness. As this practice deepens, a profound wisdom, or gnosis, begins to arise spontaneously. This is the non-dual wisdom of self-aware being. Non-dual in this case means the absence of a subject-object dichotomy. This perceived split is replaced by the insight of oneness, an experiential knowing that reality is one interdependent whole. It is this wisdom insight that many have described as "realization" or "enlightenment." It is completely beyond the mind and conceptual understanding, yet is self-known.

Here are some examples of pointing-out instructions used in the direct-awareness style of teaching in the Great Perfection tradition. This first quote is from the famous cycle of teachings known as the Tibetan Book of the Dead. The text was discovered by Karma Lingpa (born in Tibet around 1329). It was considered to have been originally written by eighth-century Master Padmasambhava, who hid the text before he left Tibet. It was later discovered by Karma Lingpa. It is part of what is called "The Direct Introduction to Awareness" teaching of Dzogchen and is meant to "awaken" those who simply read and understand the text without need for any prior or subsequent practice:

> And in the present moment, when your mind remains in its own condition without constructing anything, Awareness, at that moment, in itself is quite ordinary.
>
> And when you look into yourself in this way nakedly, without any discursive thoughts,
>
> Since there is only this pure observing, there will be found a lucid clarity without anyone being there who is the observer, only a naked manifest awareness is present.
>
> This Awareness is empty and immaculately pure, not being created by anything whatsoever. It is authentic and unadulterated, without any duality of clarity and emptiness. (From John Reynolds's translation, *Self-Liberation Through Seeing With Naked Awareness.*)

Above is the initial introduction to the nature of mind, our true nature. This is the most important experiential insight that becomes the basis of all further development of profound wisdom and realization.

Next we describe a means of integrating our energies into this pure Awareness, so that we have a realization of the non-dual nature of our total experience.

Fourteenth-century Dzogchen Master Longchenpa was one of the most accomplished Dzogchen teachers of all time. He made every effort to make these teachings available and understandable for every person according to their current capacity to comprehend. That means he had many different ways of communicating these teachings.

> In this case what makes perfect sense in the Ati (Dzogchen) approach is the superior realization whereby one directly experiences the unobstructed state in it's nakedness, without relying on anything whatsoever. Since one does not experience separation from the essence of Awareness even for an instant, to say that it is realized or perceived is merely to use a conventional expression...
>
> Awareness abides as the aspect which is aware under any and all circumstances, and so occurs naturally, without transition or change...

Longchenpa shares how to apply these teachings as well:

> The method is directing attention upon attention or awareness. When any arising is experienced, especially thoughts, moods, emotions, or feelings of personal self-identity, one simply notices one's present naked awareness. By *directing the attention* back to awareness, the arising dissolves back into its origin and its essential nature, awareness. In doing this, the **arising releases its formative energy** in its dissolution **as a surge of further clarity of Clear Light**, the *power and potency of awareness that energized the arising in the first place.*

Hence one's Awareness presence is enhanced in the collapse of the formative arising. Hence the Dzogchen comment that "the stronger the afflictive emotion upon dissolution, the stronger the enhancement to the clarity of presence. (From *A Treasure Trove of Scriptural Transmission*, Padma Publications)

Longchenpa is pointing to our basic consciousness as mind, which has an energy or power of attention. It can empower thoughts, emotions, inner sensations, sense of self and stories into momentary existence. Instead of directing our attention on our thoughts or perceptual experience, we focus our attention back on the quality of our mind that is simply being aware of all experience. When we do this in the midst of a thought or any kind of internal mental event such as uncomfortable emotions or feelings, the action of directing our attention back on our witnessing awareness causes the mental event to collapse or dissipate into its origin. As this dissolution occurs, we experience a further surge of our own sense of vivid presence. We also can do this when in a "selfing" mode, where our sense of personal and separate selfhood is dominating our cognitive experience. In this moment it's "all about me." In this case we notice the underlying awareness that is experiencing even this sense of *me* as it appears in consciousness. As we work with this practice, we may come to notice that our awareness is always unchangingly present and aware. Recognizing that we are this unchanging, knowing awareness is the basis of realization. So here we have a complete methodology of how one works within the context of the direct awareness, Great Perfection teachings.

Dzogchen master Jamgon Kongtrul Rinpoche wrote:

Why chase after thoughts, which are superficial ripples of present awareness? Rather look directly into the naked, empty nature of thoughts; then there is no duality, no observer, and nothing observed.

Simply rest in this transparent, nondual present awareness. Make yourself at home in the natural state of pure presence, just being, not doing anything in particular.

From the Dzogchen root Tantra (scriptural text), Kunje Gyalpo:

The nature of enlightenment is that of space.

There is no effort or achievement in space.

Enlightenment, which is like space, will not come about for those who indulge in effort and achievement.

"Free and Easy," by Tibetan Dzogchen master, Lama Gendun:

Happiness cannot be found through great effort and willpower, but is already present in open relaxation and letting go.

Don't strain yourself—there is nothing to do or undo. Whatever arises momentarily in the body-mind has no real importance at all, has little reality whatsoever. Why identify with it and become attached to it, passing judgment upon it and ourselves?

Far better to simply let the entire game happen on its own, springing up and falling back like waves—without changing or manipulating anything—and notice how everything vanishes and reappears, magically, again and again, time without end.

Only our searching for happiness prevents us from seeing it. It's like a vivid rainbow which you pursue without ever catching, or a dog chasing its own tail.

Although peace and happiness do not exist as an actual thing or place, it is always available and accompanies you every instant.

Don't believe in the reality of good and bad experiences; they are like today's ephemeral weather, like rainbows in the sky.

Wanting to grasp the ungraspable, you exhaust yourself in vain. As soon as you open and relax this tight fist of grasping, infinite space is here—open, inviting and comfortable.

Make use of the spaciousness, this freedom and natural ease. Don't search any further. Don't go into the tangled jungle looking for the great awakened elephant that is already resting quietly at home in front of your own hearth.

Nothing to do or undo,

Nothing to force,

Nothing to want, and

Nothing missing.

Emaho! Marvelous!

Everything happens by itself.

The second school of Tibetan Buddhism that offers a direct-awareness style of teaching is called *Mahamudra*. It is also works on the basis of a teacher "pointing out" directly the nature of enlightened mind to the student in the context of a one-on-one encounter. In fact, the ancient style of transmitting the pointing-out instruction was done by the master singing a song of phrases called *dohas*, which directly caused the student's mind to awaken into enlightenment. These teachings were maintained in total secrecy, but now they are relatively accessible to seekers worldwide. However, the system of Mahamudra today is almost always taught within the context of a two-step program of gradual meditation. The goal is first to bring the mind to a state of quiet stillness called calm abiding. In this phase of practice one discovers the nature of thoughts to be like transparent clouds floating in the sky of one's own awareness. The thoughts are seen to arise from emptiness and dissolve again into emptiness. One's concentration develops in such a way that one is no longer distracted by the various thoughts that continuously arise and dissolve from moment to moment. It is not necessarily true that all thinking ceases but rather the thoughts no longer have the power to attract one's clarity of attention into their alluring stories. We can simply remain relaxed and fully alert in here-and-now presence of awareness.

The second phase of Mahamudra meditation deals with utilizing our clarity of awareness to observe the origins of thought, the nature of thought, and the nature of personal identity as defined by our thoughts. It is within this period of non-conceptual observing that one may discover the ephemeral nature of our sense of self or identity. If a profound insight arises in this regard, it may reveal the enlightened awareness that has always otherwise gone unnoticed. This insight then blossoms into the realization that all of reality is the expression of Being, the realization known as Mahamudra, which means "great symbol or gesture." The symbol is our total world, and the gesture is pointing to its inseparable source as Knowing Being. This would then be the realization of the fruit of Mahamudra practice. If this realization didn't arise within the context of the student's own meditation practice, the teacher would engage in guided meditations directing the student's attention to various aspects of his or her thought processes, consciousness, and aware presence. This continues between the teacher and the student until the student has a "breakthrough" insight. When it is clear the student has authentic insight regarding the recognition of the enlightened nature, he or she is instructed the same as is done in Dzogchen, which is to simply continue in that newly exposed state of naked observingness.

It's important to realize that in Zen, Dzogchen, Mahamudra, and Advaita teachings, there is no concept of someone "achieving" enlightenment or an enlightened state. Rather it is simply *recognizing* that one's awareness has always been fully enlightened and then living as the awareness he or she has always been but did not recognize. In Mahamudra, that condition is also called the *natural state*. It is our primordial condition, which never changes, like the sky never changes while all the changing clouds and weather come and go.

I should mention there is also a more ancient teaching lineage of Mahamudra called Essence Mahamudra. It has no sense of gradual realization or attainment through practices. The most famous masters of this unique tradition were Saraha, Maitripa, and Tilopa. All were from India and lived more than one thousand years ago. As time went by their teachings became incorporated into a more gradual approach utilizing both yogic energy practices and simple meditation methods dealing with various aspects of the mind. Here are some quotes from masters of Essence Mahamudra:

Kalu Rinpoche:

> Mind is poised in the state of bare awareness, there is no directing the mind. One is not looking within for anything; one is not looking without for anything.

One is simply letting the mind rest in its own natural state. The empty, clear and unimpeded nature of mind can be experienced if we can rest in an uncontrived state of bare awareness without distraction and without the spark of awareness being lost.

From Niguma, the great female master of Mahamudra:

Don't bring anything to mind,

Be it real or imagined.

Rest uncontrived in the innate state.

Your own mind, uncontrived, is the body of ultimate enlightenment.

To remain undistracted within this, is meditation's essential point.

Realize the great, boundless, expansive state.

From Maitripa:

Clarity without thought is like space.

Appearances, without substance, are like the moon on water.

Clarity without clinging is like a rainbow.

Like a young lover's pleasure, it is indescribable. This is not localized and exceeds all bounds.

From Tilopa:

Don't recall.

Don't imagine.

Don't think.

Don't analyze.

Don't control.

Rest.

There is also a non-Buddhist tradition that also offers a "sudden insight" approach called Advaita. Its teachings can be traced to the ancient Indian Vedas and Upanishads. The Advaita enlightenment known as self-realization can be transmitted by a teacher directly as is done in Zen and Dzogchen. Students dialogue with a teacher, either in a one-on-one meeting or a group meeting called a *Satsang*. However, pure Advaita per se does not offer any particular meditation methods or practices beyond self-inquiry. In this way its philosophical position is similar to Dzogchen in that it is understood that one's enlightened awareness is already fully present. It is only the seeking ego that blocks our knowing of what is already the natural condition of our being. We need to get out of the way of ourselves, so to speak, and no practice or meditation is needed for that, just a clear insight into what's going on. That insight is catalyzed by direct discussion with an Advaita teacher or by reading and studying some pith instructions by various Advaita masters. In recent times two great teachers of Advaita have written and taught extensively on the topic. One is Nisargadatta and the other is Ramana Maharshi. Both are from India and have since passed away. Students can gain wonderful and profound insights from reading their pithy quotes and texts.

Both Advaita and Dzogchen in that sense are relying on the intrinsic wisdom already fully present within our own consciousness. No practices are required to recognize this wisdom because practices and methods are only further interferences with the direct perception that recognizes itself. To do a practice one needs a doer of the practice. In Advaita this is a key teaching. To engage in practice is considered empowering the ego, the imaginary doer, further in its various activities of grasping and striving for some ultimate state of bliss or enlightenment. When the ego as the mind's sense of personal identity falls away, all that's left is enlightened Awareness, our actual beingness, which has been there all the time. As Awareness, we were just expressing a moment of ego experience as another variety of experience. As an aside, there is a Western phrase I heard in recent times: "Its not that we are a humans having spiritual experiences, but rather we are spiritual beings having human experiences."

Below are quotes from two twentieth-century Advaita masters:

Awareness is ever there. It need not be realized. Open the shutter of the mind, and it will be flooded with light.

First we must know ourselves as witnesses only, dimensionless and timeless centers of observation, and then realize that immense ocean of pure awareness which is both mind and matter and beyond both.

The personality gives place to the witness, then the witness goes and pure awareness remains.

There are no steps to self-realization. There is nothing gradual about it. It happens suddenly and is irreversible. Just like at sunrise you see things as they are, so at self-realization you see everything as it is. The world of illusions is left behind.

Put your awareness to work, not your mind. The mind is not the right instrument for this task. The timeless can be reached only by the timeless. Your body and your mind are born subject to time; only awareness is timeless, even in the now. (From: I Am That, by Sri Nisargadatta Maharaj. Published by Chetana, Bombay, 1992)

Ramana Maharshi:

You are awareness. Awareness is another name for you.

Since you are awareness there is no need to attain or cultivate it.

Questioner: How can I tell if I am making progress with my enquiry?

The degree of the absence of thoughts is the measure of your progress towards Self-Realization. But Self-Realization itself does not admit of progress, it is ever the same. The Self remains always in realization. The obstacles are thoughts. Progress is measured by the degree of removal of the obstacles to understanding that the Self is always realized. So thoughts must be checked by seeking to *whom* they arise. So you go to their source, where they do not arise.

Next we have a few quotes from the Zen tradition that relate to the direct-awareness approach.

Fukanzazengi by Eihei Dogen, of the Soto Zen sect, thirteenth-century Japan:

The Way is in essence perfect and pervades everywhere. How could it be dependent upon what anyone does to practice or realize it? The movement of Reality does not need us to give it a push. Do I need to say that it is free from delusion? The vast expanse of Reality can never be darkened by the dust of presumptions. Who then could believe that it needs to be cleaned of such dust to be what it is? It is never separate from where you are, so why scramble around in search of it?

You should therefore cease from practice based on intellectual understanding, pursuing words and following after speech, and learn the backward step that turns your light inwardly to illuminate your self. Body and mind of themselves will drop away, and your original face will be manifest. If you want to attain Suchness (True Nature), you should practice Suchness (Being your True Nature) without delay.

My comment:

Reality is already breathing us, thinking us, and living us. There is nothing special for us to do except whatever we are doing. Whichever way you turn, you are always facing the right direction. Everything is exactly where it should be. Who else could you be if not yourself?

In Korean Zen, as shared in the twelfth-century works of Chinul, there is a method that is used to enter the awakened state directly. It is the eighth method as listed in the most profound ten methods of direct entry.

Zen Master Chinul writes:

> Internal and external are all the same function. That means when we are practicing, we take up all the phenomena of the physical universe, internal, external, mental or physical as well as motion and activity, and regard them all as the sublime activity of the True Mind (Awareness). As soon as any thought or mental state arises, it is then the appearance of this sublime function. Since all things are this sublime functioning, where can the deluded mind stand? This is the method of extinguishing delusion by seeing that all things external and internal are the same function of the True Mind (Awareness). (From *The Collected Works of Chinul, The Korean Approach to Zen,* translated by Robert E. Buswell Jr.)

You will often hear teachers say that the problem is that "we have identified ourselves as being this body or personality." Somehow it is conceived that what we are has the capacity to err and stray into this mistaken process of identification. The *we* being referred to is our original pure state of being. But if we actually look deeply into this original state, we won't be able to find anything there that "identifies" itself with anything at all.

We could use the example of changeless space. Birds, clouds, planets, and stars all appear in space yet not in any way separate from that space. We can't conceive of a bird flying outside of the space of its appearance. But we can conceive of empty space without the appearance of a bird. The space has not become a bird but rather always remains in its own dimension of emptiness. Likewise our true original pure state of being, expressed as being a knowing awareness, has never become a "something" but always remains in its dimension of emptiness. But like space, all manner of things can appear in this empty space of "knowing awareness". Consider the glass of a mirror as appearing to be interpenetrated by reflections, yet the glass remains unchanged. The reflections have no existence outside of the mirror, but the clear glass of the mirror is not dependent on the reflections in any way.

Consider the sense of identification like the thought and feeling, "I am this body." This is a complete experience in itself. In other words, this thought and feeling is one entire package of information appearing like a reflection in the mirror of awareness. It is not that there is an *unchanging I* that then becomes identified with the thought of being this body, but rather the thought of "I" and the thought "am this body" are just one complete sentence or image appearing in awareness. Awareness has never conceived of itself as either an "I" or "being this body." Likewise, the glass of a mirror never becomes its reflections, yet all manner of reflections appear. On a more subtle level, the same is true with identification as a personality. The mind conceives a self-image, our sense of character and personhood. This conceptual construction also is just an appearance in the always empty space of awareness.

Whatever thought, concept, or image you can conceive regarding personal identity never affects the empty space of knowing awareness in which they appear. Yet we can't find any distance or separation from that empty space of knowing awareness regarding those conceptions. Similarly, there is no separation between the waves and the water in which they take shape. But also the nature of the water is not altered by whatever shapes the waves assume.

So hopefully, after personally looking into this in a moment of quiet contemplation, we see that our empty knowing awareness never identifies itself as being anything all, yet the thoughts of being this or that arise and dissolve constantly in this changeless space of original being. That being the case, of what benefit could a philosophy or spiritual practice offer regarding realization? Whatever thoughts or spiritual experiences appear, they are never more than empty appearances arising in the empty and changeless space of awareness. We have never left that original state of being as the empty space of knowing awareness in which all appearances appear. Your current empty knowing awareness is where the experience of *being a person reading these words* is appearing in. Experience, beliefs, confusions, identities, and appearances are never as content, a problem for the *context* in which they appear.

However, in actual practice many unprepared people don't experience this immediate and profoundly transformative realization. They may have great epiphanies and mystical insights, but they tend eventually to regress to some degree. Therefore it seems that a firm foundation of meditation practice and gradual development of insight is recommended to assist the ripening as one enters these direct-awareness paths. The make-or-break point determining likely or unlikely success seems to be dependent on whether the student's false sense of self-identification has been released or deconstructed previously.

However, for some the direct-awareness approach is just exactly the right teaching at the right time. In all cases there needs to be a dialogue between a student and a teacher so the teacher can assess the best way to proceed. As a teacher, I always begin with the direct-awareness approach with students. By their response to this effort to catalyze some fundamental shift in consciousness, I am able to assess what exactly needs to be done next. It may be a very short program of practice or meditation to get the mind better prepared. Then we continue the efforts of bringing about a sudden shift in consciousness that can be more stable and is likely to blossom into ever greater depths of insight.

The second approach to self-realization is the gradual path of meditation. It focuses on the body, inner energy, mind, and the mind's activities. The goal is at first to assist the mind to come to a calmer and clearer state. This means reducing the volume of thought and the tendency to develop our thoughts into the various stories that arise from focusing on our mind's messages and images. There are literally hundreds of meditation methods and practices from which to choose. But they all come down to two basic components: calming the mind and increasing insight.

To give a general overview of a foundational practice, let's examine a basic description of meditation. Basic meditation is comprised of sitting on a cushion on the floor or on a chair, but in both cases you should try to keep your spine straight, yet not tense. You can arrange your hands comfortably on your thighs or knees. At first, you can close your eyes and focus on noticing your incoming and outgoing breath. After a few minutes, open your eyes and focus on a point on the floor about four or five feet in front. Try to keep your eyes still, but it is okay to blink. Notice your breathing as before. Your focus is on the point on the floor, but especially notice the feeling of the air passing in and out of your nostrils and the filling and emptying of the lungs as you breathe naturally. If you seem a little dreamy and full of thoughts, focus your concentration a bit more. If you feel agitated, make the room darker or close your eyes and try to slow your breathing with much deeper and slower out breaths. Find a comfortable balance between the right amount of focus and the right amount of looseness.

When you focus your eyes on a point or small object in front of you, it actually slows down your stream of thought. This has been noted by neuroscientists studying the effects of meditation. Taking slow, full deep breaths and expanding your lungs to full capacity for several minutes stimulates cells called baro-receptors in the lung tissue. This triggers the parasympathetic nervous system to release chemicals that neutralize the effects of adrenaline, producing real relaxation on a biological level. Slow deep breathing for ten minutes or so stops or lessens panic attacks as well. A key element of breath practice is to make sure the out-breath is much slower than the in-breath.

You should have no mental agenda in mind when meditating. You should not be thinking of reducing thinking. You are just observing, like a mirror or video camera. A video camera has no ability to judge or analyze what it records. Just sit in pure observingness. If there is any effort, let it be the subtle preference of being in the "now" of immediate sensory experience, as opposed to drifting off into thoughts and daydreams. If you are too tired to be in a state of natural and relaxed mental clarity, take a nap and try again. Don't fight sleepiness; it's usually a waste of time. If you are too agitated to sit peacefully, take a walk and try again later. When your mind is too busy, it can be helpful to focus on noticing your breathing and mentally count your breaths from one to ten again and again until you're calmer. At that point, drop the counting and just remain aware of your breathing. When your mind becomes quiet and almost still, you can drop the focus on breathing and just float in vivid and alert "now-ness." This state is called naked awareness; the awareness is not clothed in thoughts, mental images, or emotional states. We simply reside as this naked awareness and continue in this condition after our sitting session for as long as possible. Our goal is to allow that naked awareness to be our normal basis of cognitive life throughout the day and night. Thoughts, mental images, and emotional states will arise, but they are experienced from the perspective of our naked awareness instead of our being subjectively centered in our stories.

If you find that a particular mental topic or group of topics keep appearing annoyingly in your mind, there is a way to dissolve the mental distraction. As you notice your breathing, imagine on the in-breath that the thought in your mind, like a little cloud of thought energy in your head, joins up with your breath at your nose, exits with the out-breath, and dissolves into the space in front of you. Then on the in-breath, notice if you have another thought in your mind, and repeat the process until the troublesome thoughts no longer remain in your mind.

A sitting meditation session should last twenty to forty minutes. If meditating as I've described is very difficult, you can work up to twenty minutes with five-minute sessions and a short break between each if necessary. I recommend daily sessions while giving this practice outline a try.

Advaita master Nisargadatta recommends:

> As long as you are a beginner certain formalized meditations, or prayers, may be good for you. But for a seeker for reality there is only one meditation; the rigorous refusal to harbor thoughts. To be free from thoughts is itself meditation. You begin by letting thoughts flow and watching them. The very observation slows down the mind till it stops altogether. Once the mind is quiet, keep it quiet. Don't get bored with peace, be in it, go deeper into it.... Watch your thoughts and *watch yourself watching the thoughts*. The state of freedom from all thoughts will happen suddenly and by the bliss of it you shall recognise it. (From *I Am That*, by Sri Nisargadatta Maharaj. Published by Chetana, Bombay, 1992.)

Now let's discuss the benefits of the gradual approach to realization. First, you tend to have more stability and retain its benefits longer. This is due to the neuro-plasticity of the brain. That means the brain is moldable and pliable. Neuroscience used to think that our brains were set and fundamentally unchanging from childhood on. Now we know different. The brain adapts to different stimuli and experiences. We know from MRI and brain-scan research that over as little as eight weeks, the brain shows physical changes after daily meditation of forty-five minutes per session. The areas of the brain that are associated with generating calmness and clarity develop more visible activity, and the areas associated with anxiety, depression, and stress show reductions in neural activity. By engaging in calming meditations over a period of time, the neural circuitry that establishes those patterns of cognitive experience gradually increases in the zones of the brain we want to develop, and it decreases in the areas we wish to deactivate. Measurable increases in "gray matter" are detectable in those areas that are beneficial to a positive state of mind, such as in the hippocampus. Long-term meditators have noticeably different brain scans than non-meditators. The areas of the brain associated with positive states of mind show a full and deep level of activation. Even without having meditated recently, the changes tend to remain. The baseline of normal brain activity rises to a positive state, along with detectable long-term positive changes in brain tissue. We can literally rewire our brain's circuitry. So if you want to reduce current levels of anxiety and stress, meditation is a proven method. Likewise if you want to experience more positive states of mind and moods, again, meditation is the best solution I know of.

Recent breakthroughs in MRI or brain-scan technology have been able to locate the main areas of the brain associated with self-focused activity, what could be called "selfing." Selfing means that we are not just engaged in a mental or physical activity but along with the mental or physical activity in which we are engaged comes an overriding sense of *me* as a self-referencing self-consciousness. However when these areas of the brain are not active, our experience is quite different. Life and experience just flow in a natural and spontaneous way, almost effortlessly.

Some have described this state as being "in the zone" or in "a state of flow." High-performance athletes describe this state as occurring during moments requiring total focus and clarity. In these moments, they say there is a total absence of self-consciousness as the body just seems to follow its own innate intelligence.

Stress, depression, and anxiety are associated with these various selfing centers of the brain. When the sense of ego or "me" is strongly pervading our overall experience, it poisons the water, so to speak. The brain creates this sense of *I*, of being a separate self through the interaction of several areas of the brain associated with the "selfing" mechanism. It is probably some kind of feedback loop that evolved within the species to allow more self-referencing regarding the survival and social implications of various actions. It's probably also directly associated with our fear and hesitation before engaging in new and adventurous activity. Perhaps "selfing" has outlived its value in our species; however, its predominance has not. It seems directly driven by an organism's urge for its *self* to survive. This one isn't going to go away easily or quietly unless we reprogram the software and hardware of the brain. Meditation can help do just that.

On the other hand, when individuals experience deeply transformative states of consciousness, as occurs in realization, much of the brain's software is reprogrammed regarding selfing and its attendant mechanisms. It's as though the brain and mind have a reset button that not only can realign the overall cognitive systems of the individual but tend to upgrade the entire system into a new way of processing information and experience.

Two levels of cognitive consciousness seem possible. One appears to act as a computer that follows the laws of classical Newtonian physics. It assesses and processes information on a purely biological stimulus-and-response basis. The other functions much more like a "quantum computer" that works on different principles of information accessing, processing, and distribution. A later chapter discusses this new topic of "quantum consciousness" and how the brain appears to have both a computing ability along quantum lines as well as along classical computing principles. More advanced forms of meditation seem to activate the quantum aspects of the brain and mind, hence our interest in understanding this fascinating new field where neuroscience, spirituality, and quantum physics meet. Through this quantum aspect of consciousness, our non-material, spiritual nature interfaces with the body and brain.

A variety of meditation practices for beginners and those more advanced are available in the appendix with complete instructions for practice.

The third approach to self-realization comprises a variety of methods called energy practices, which are similar to yoga with its breathing exercises and inner visualizations. In this approach, we work with very subtle energies that flow throughout our bodies and brains and influence our states of consciousness. This subtle energy has been called life force, prana, or chi, depending on which tradition we speak from. Acupuncture is based completely on repairing and harmonizing the circulation of this life force energy through subtle channels that often follow major nerve pathways and nerve complexes in the body. This life force energy is called *chi* in Chinese. The energy practices can be very grounding and can dissolve subtle energy blockages associated with many unwanted mental and emotional states that are the major sources of our suffering.

Too often in my experience, I have found that Western seekers try to "think" their way to enlightenment. Often the cognitive impediments blocking realization are grounded in blockages and imbalances within the inner subtle body. These seekers may have brilliant intellectual insights that may be quite convincing, but they are almost always short-lived. The mind reverts to a pattern embedded deeply within the inner energy body until those patterns are released and transformed. For those who want to practice very simple energy practices, the appendix contains a gradient of practices that anyone could find useful.

If you approach enlightenment from the direct-awareness approach, you still have the full sensory experience that results from the energy practices, but their effect won't be as dramatic. Likewise, by doing the energy practices alone, all of the intuitive insights experienced in the direct-awareness approach also occur. When I was studying Sufism in Kashmir in 1978, I asked my teacher if it was necessary to use the yogic-like energy body practices or was it sufficient just doing the direct awareness meditations without concern for body postures etc. He said either is fine and that both approaches lead to the same result. I preferred the mind-only approach and wasted many years lost in my concepts and temporary insights. Years later, when I began the subtle energy body practices in earnest, everything came to completion quite quickly. There may be a lesson for others in this.

In order to fully understand the energy practices, it might be good to place the topic in context. In most cultures, there are religious traditions that believe a human is not just a physical body but also a spiritual nature that survives death. That which survives death is most commonly called the soul. Each spiritual tradition has its own description of the soul and its life after death. We won't be going into great detail about the specifics of any particular tradition's story-line associated with the after-world, but we will explore teachings regarding the nature of the soul itself. In the Eastern traditions, especially the teachings of Hindu yoga and Tibetan Buddhism, there exists a rich and detailed explanation of the subtle inner body, the energy structure of what is often called the soul. It is taught that this energy body survives death and reincarnates again and again. It is this subtle energy body that is the vehicle for one's consciousness after death. It is considered to be the life force, the *élan vital*, of the physical body. Some traditions consider the soul to be an entity that is permanent, independent, and autonomous. In Buddhism the notion is of an impermanent continuum of consciousness, not a fixed entity or self. But liberation or realization lies beyond both concepts of there being a fixed entity or a continuum of consciousness. The innermost essence of consciousness as pure awareness is without any sense of a fixed entity or a continuum. It is beyond all categories of thought and description and must be known directly by awareness in a moment of recognizing itself.

By understanding and learning to work with the energies within this subtle body, it is quite easy to bring about a state of profound spiritual insight. One of the greatest benefits to working with the inner energies of the subtle body is that we can bring the mind to total stillness quite easily and swiftly. In this condition you are more likely to recognize the essential nature of awareness, the already enlightened consciousness that we seek to reveal. However, I wish to make it abundantly clear that it is *not* necessary for most individuals to engage in the yogic-like meditation practices or the methods concerning the inner subtle body. We are discussing this as an optional and auxiliary method for those so inclined.

Many students prefer working with the subtle energy body more than just the cognitive aspects of the mind. On the other hand, many individuals who are more intellectually oriented have no interest in the energy practices. That said, I still think it is good information for anyone interested in self-realization and spiritual development. The experiences that occur by engaging in these basic energy practices bring an understanding that is completely beyond intellectual conceptualization and wishful thinking. This is important, as most Westerners overemphasize the intellectual aspects of the search for spiritual wisdom and enlightenment. On the other hand, ego-mind can also go overboard trying to grasp experiences generated from these methods. Some individuals become attached to amazing experiences of bliss, great clarity or an empty mind state that translate into chronic efforts to relive experiences that were merely signposts or passing milestones along the way. So if one is so inclined, it is good to find a balance between the approaches of either simply resting in alert presence of awareness or developing greater clarity through yogic practices. In Tibet, the greatest masters recommended combining both approaches in daily practice, at least in the beginning stages.

Let's take a look at the anatomy of the subtle inner body, which will be relevant to our practice. The pattern I discuss is essentially the same in traditions such as Tibetan Buddhism, Yoga, Zen, Taoism, Sufism, Kabbalah, and Native American traditions. To begin with, the traditions teach that we have an inner energy that flows through subtle channels in the body. This inner energy has many different names depending upon the tradition. In Yoga, this energy is called *prana*. In Tibetan Buddhism, it is called *lung* or "energy wind." In Taoism and traditional Chinese medicine, it is called *chi* and is the main focus of acupuncture, as I mentioned above. In Japanese Zen and martial arts, it is called *ki*. The most universally used term is probably prana, from the Hindu Yoga traditions. However, I will use the model for the architecture of the inner body as described mostly from the Tibetan traditions.

As already mentioned, prana or chi is an energy that flows throughout our bodies within subtle channels called *nadi*. There are three main channels or nadi in the subtle body that we use in yogic meditation practice. The most important in all traditions is the central channel. It runs along the spine, some say *within* the spinal column, from its base of the spine up to the crown or fontanel at the top of the skull. We refer to this energy pathway as the central channel. On both sides of the central channel is a side channel that runs parallel to the spine. These channels arise from a location just above the base of the spine. Along the central channel are several energy centers that are the focus of all subtle body functions and are somewhat comparable to the physical body's internal organs.

As per the Yoga tradition we will call those energy centers *chakras.* At the bottom of the spine is the root chakra. Going up to a place adjacent to one's navel is the navel chakra. Going farther up is the heart chakra. Above the heart chakra is the throat chakra. At the upper part of the crown of the head, just below the fontanel, is the crown chakra. At a space between and just above the eyes is another chakra called the third-eye chakra. It is the place where Hindus often place a red dot on their foreheads, called a *bindu.* For Hindus it is known as the *ajna* chakra. Other traditions may mention additional chakras, but those mentioned here are sufficient for our practice. When these chakras are fully activated, the individual experiences corresponding changes in consciousness. This is why we are discussing the subtle body; we are interested in the states of consciousness that result from specific chakra activation.

For example, when the crown chakra is fully activated and "opened," your mind becomes absolutely devoid of thought activity and any sense of personal ego or self. You experience your consciousness as a crystal clear state of vivid awareness. Your awareness seems no longer limited by your body; it feels boundless, without borders or a specific center. It's accompanied by a sense of authentic, indestructible *beingness* that can't be conditioned by experience. As this awareness, you are suffused with the pure joy of total freedom and oneness with all existence. This is the experience of non-duality and is the true nature of our existence. The experience cannot be denied as your intrinsic certainty and vivid clarity overshadow all limited frameworks constructed by the conceptualizing mind. It is this gnosis or essential realization to which we aspire in our practice. Our authentic or natural state of realized awareness will arise spontaneously; at first occasionally until total stability occurs.

Teaching these subtle energy body practices over the years, I have found that most people easily enter the initial phases of crown chakra activation. Most people will experience a significant shift in consciousness during the first practice session. I will be sharing methods in this chapter that you can apply easily, but first we need to complete our map of the subtle body and its energy components and processes. I recommend that those with significant experience in these topics and practices with the inner energy body, take a fresh look at what I am sharing here. There is much false and confusing information in the market place of *supposed* spiritual knowledge being taught and sold.

The methods I am sharing in this book produce the desired effects when followed exactly as described. But to be fair to the material, I recommend leaving prior information and teaching regarding the subtle body aside for the moment. Otherwise, unnecessary complications from trying to make correlations between prior knowledge and what I am sharing may occur. This could inhibit the effectiveness of the methods being discussed. So with that in mind, let's proceed further with our understanding of the subtle body and its energy processes.

We have already discussed the five key chakras: the root chakra at the base of the spine, the navel chakra, the heart chakra, the throat chakra, the crown chakra, and the third-eye chakra. They are centralized around the central channel as their axis. The center point of each chakra is within the central channel, including the third-eye chakra. The central channel extends along the spine from its base to the fontanel and then curves forward and down, with an opening at the third-eye chakra.

The right and left channels run parallel to the central channel from just below the navel chakra upward into the crown. From there they bend forward to terminate at the nostrils, the right channel at the right nostril and the left channel at the left nostril. Consider that the two side channels are connected and enter into the central channel at a place just below the navel chakra. The side channels play almost no role in our energy practice, but it is good to know about them because they account for certain energy experiences you may notice during our practice.

The most subtle of all inner energies exists within the central channel as pure consciousness. Therefore if your mind experiences its own most essential nature, your mind will be totally clear and present in the absence of all mental activities. It is this clear-and-present awareness state that we are looking to reveal. It's also known as the *clear light* in Tibetan traditions. The subtle energy circulating in the two side channels is a conditioned mental energy that ensnares the mind by enlivening ego-related thought patterns and concepts. The practice is to merge the energies in the side channels into the central channel at the entry point just below the navel chakra. As these "impure" energies enter the central channel, they are immediately purified and transformed into pure consciousness. As a practice, you can visualize how the side channels connect to the central channel and attempt to draw their inner energies into the central channel. Or you can simply focus on the center point of any one of the five chakras. This focusing on the center point of any chakra will cause the energy from the side channels to enter the central channel at that chakra automatically. This specific practice is the mainstay of the Hindu and Buddhist Tantric practices that have been taught to students for more than 1,500 years. I received these teachings from both Hindu and Tibetan Buddhist masters.

Going further with our model of the subtle energy body, it is important to understand why we are so interested in developing this inner energy in the first place. There is a very concentrated subtle energy mostly located at the base of the spine known as *kundalini*. In Tibetan it is called *thigle*. It is a very pure form of chi or prana. Kundalini is also located in the center of all the chakras with an abundance at the center of the crown chakra. The entire goal of the subtle energy body practices is to activate kundalini energy at the base of the spine and bring it through the central channel to the crown chakra. If you imagine the crown chakra as the blossom of a lotus flower and the central channel as the stem of the lotus, you could consider the kundalini as the sap that rises from the roots of the lotus at the base of the spine to the blossom at the top. Normally the lotus is closed and the sap doesn't flow upward. But in these practices we encourage the upward flow of the sap into the lotus blossom that causes the blossom to fully open. In Hindu yoga the crown chakra is considered to have one thousand petals. When the crown chakra opens fully, you experience total enlightenment automatically.

I would like to share an early experience I had many years ago with the subtle body energy practices and kundalini activation. It had a permanent effect on how I experience the universe around me. Here are my notes from that time:

> Through recent study and practices of Taoist yoga
> that emphasized the "crown" chakra, the kundalini

did enter the crown chakra today for the first time that I can recall. The experience was unlike any state of mind that I have ever experienced...It was as though I had only experienced the fragrance or scent of Reality in past practice. In this case I was immersed in the Nature of Reality to such a degree that the Knowledge concerning Being and our true nature was instantly revealed. It was as though my head had become transparent and devoid of any mass...there was a sense of boundless spaciousness. But that spaciousness was Awareness, fully present like a witness, yet existing *as* everything. Witness as everything witnessed. It seemed as the though the universe was transparent like a hologram floating in this Clear Light Space of Awareness. Clearly I was the unchanging Presence that was completely outside of space and time. The whole mandala or environment in my house was shimmering as though transparent...the whole physical universe was exactly as it appears normally, but very, very thin as though without any real concrete substance. I could see through it into pure space.

The feeling-tone was total bliss...I mean not just feeling good...but total bliss. A deep sense of awe and primordial perfection...everything is Self-Being and everything arises within this as this. There was no trace of mind or ego...just this "Knowingness" as blissful Being.

This was early in the morning...a little later I took a shower and had an incredible experience. As the water came out of the showerhead, as it struck my skin, it seemed as though the water just passed through my body without being impeded at all. I am sure that was not the case...but that is exactly what it felt like. My head also seemed transparent as though I could see out the back as well as straight through the top. The movement of my body was experienced as almost orgasmic bliss...I would just spontaneously sway as the warm shower water penetrated every cell...only furthering the bliss.

This lasted most of the day. The next day, going to work was truly amazing. My head felt transparent and as though bathed in a cool breeze that only emphasized the sensations of spaciousness. My mind thought about nothing...there was just total presence in "now." How easy to live and work in this "state." No effort or care was needed, yet precision without intention flowed naturally. How wonderful! How easy!

For the last several days this state arises spontaneously when I am fully relaxed and present...but the intensity has dimmed. Yet the blissful feeling arises almost continuously but much more serene and even.

What is so fascinating about working directly with the *energy* of consciousness is that the energy has no interest whether you are a believer or not. You do the energy practices and the results will be the same for anyone regardless of religion, culture, or belief system. This is important for my efforts in general. I am trying to develop a completely generic approach that anyone from any culture can apply easily and effectively.

In Zen Buddhism the main practice is to just sit in the correct posture without focusing the mind on any topic other than perhaps noticing your breathing. You are usually instructed to focus attention within the navel chakra. By doing this consistently with alert concentration, the energy in the navel chakra increases to the point of overflowing downward toward the base of the spine where it will enter the central channel. From the downward pressure on the energy entering the central channel, prana will begin moving up the central channel to the crown chakra. When the energy enters the crown, true non-dual *samadhi* or meditation occurs. Ordinary ego-consciousness, which is centered in the brain and crown chakra, transforms into pure Awareness. This heralds the point of total realization. Your energetic sense of ego or contracted individual identity dissolves revealing its empty aware nature automatically, like ice melting into water. At this time an inseparability and one-ness with the universe is recognized, and you have profound insights into the nature of Reality. In the early Buddhist teach-ings, groups of texts called the Prajnaparamita Sutras state that all material forms are essentially empty of any inherently inde-pendent existence, but this emptiness expresses itself exactly as the forms we perceive. This wisdom becomes unmistakably known.

In quantum physics, a similar notion says that what we con-sider to be material objects are almost 100 percent empty space. There is no static solidity that endures as some kind of unchang-ing mass or substance. Yet this luminous emptiness fully appears as our apparently solid world. It is said that in deep meditation we realize that forms are essentially transparent emptiness, like holograms. But this emptiness is never absent of expressing itself as the forms we experience. When the crown chakra fully opens, our awareness recognizes that "form is exactly emptiness and emptiness is exactly form," as the ancient Buddhist texts describe.

A strong theory in modern quantum physics says that the entire universe is a hologram. We perceive this directly to be the actual nature of all reality, including ourselves and all beings. This is because the energy of consciousness that makes up our sense of being a material and individualized self has realized its own transparent emptiness. *Awareness is recognized to be a space-like emptiness devoid of any material substance.* When you perceive this in a moment of gnosis or spiritual insight, reflexively you understand that the entire field of experience is also a transparent energy display. Physical reality appears as an all-inclusive transparent hologram shimmering in crystal-like patterns of its own luminosity. The experiential tone is one of sheer delight, the conscious quality of its own self-knowing. This is an actual experience of "oneness" or non-duality that erupts into consciousness spontaneously and is quite beyond the ken of the intellect to grasp or imagine. In fact, this wisdom is only known when the intellect and conceptualizing mind are completely absent and inoperative.

The reason you experience oneness with all of reality, is because you are no longer one small and separate piece of reality. As long as you're *something*, you can't be *nothing*. Until you are nothing or empty awareness in experiential knowledge, you can't be everything. *The emptiness of your form is the form of your emptiness.* This is the core of the enlightened wisdom insight that occurs on the full activation of the crown chakra. We could use the example of an ice cube in a bowl of water. As an ice cube, the water has taken on the appearance of individuality. But when the ice cube melts, the identity is now the entire bowl of water. This is the enlightenment experience. You are this vast and borderless ocean of pure consciousness that appears as this or that apparent form. But ultimately all forms are just forms of consciousness; the ice cube is never not the formless water.

As noted earlier, I give full instructions on the subtle energy body practices in the appendix. But here I will give an overview of the initial process and methodology.

First, you need to sit in an upright position. You can do this while sitting a bit forward on a chair so as to get the posture of the spine as straight as possible. I prefer sitting on a cushion on the floor yoga style. How you arrange your legs is not so important; just be in a stable position. Rest your hands comfortably on your legs as you like. Your spine must be straight.

Close your eyes and notice your breathing. Feel the breath as it passes in and out of your nose, and notice how your lungs expand and relax with each breath.

Next, sense the central channel running from the bottom of your spine to the fontanel. You don't have to visualize it clearly, just sense that there is an energy channel running in the spinal column from bottom to top. Focus on the top most point of your head, slightly behind the center of the skull. You can locate the fontanel with your finger. It may feel like a small indentation or soft spot on the skull. Imagine an energy center there that vibrates subtly at the fontanel, perhaps an inch or two below, within the brain. At some point your attention settles on this correct location naturally, so don't worry about getting it just right. Just focus on the general area. Once you sense some sort of energy movement that holds your attention, you have located the crown chakra. Now focus on that energy point for as long as comfortable, at least five minutes or so. Remember, you don't have to visualize or imagine anything, just focus your attention on the general location.

The crown chakra is present in everyone; you just have to notice it. Once you notice it, it should feel like a slight vibration or energy pulsation. Keep that as your point of reference. Try to keep your attention on that point as often as possible through-out the day and evening, especially when about to fall asleep. Try to do twenty minutes of sitting meditation every day with only this practice. Once you have success in locating the crown chakra, your meditation should bring about a slightly altered state of consciousness, more relaxed and calm. At times you feel like you could remain focused on the crown chakra or fontanel for hours because it's so pleasant. By all means, continue as long as it's comfortable. A key aspect of practice is to allow tension to release and to find total relaxation of body and mind. By relaxing completely yet remaining vividly alert, the inner channels and chakras open fully, allowing a very pleasant sensation to pervade the entire body. Your state of mind will be expansive and serene. By engaging in the practice as described above, the entire inner subtle energy body becomes toned and activated. Again, this is just a brief introduction to the energy body practices. A complete description along with some initial preparatory exercises that may be necessary are in the appendix titled "The Main Subtle Body Practice Sequence."

Let's summarize and bring all three of these approaches into a relational context. At first, you may try to find your enlightened nature within your own consciousness. You may receive a pointing-out instruction regarding the nature of changeless awareness. However, you may only understand intellectually that your identity is not the body or mind. But there is no total shift in perspective. This gives you a certain degree of relaxation, as though the intellect has acquired its goal of understanding and can now relax. But that intellectual insight does not drive deep enough into the energy contraction remaining in the subtle body and physical body, so it is short-lived. There was just a flash of insight but no total transformation of the self-contraction and mind. By recognizing that subtle flash again and again, and learning to rest in the naked observing-ness in all experience, thoughts and mental engagement become calmer and less captivating. As a result your inner subtle body of chakras, channels, and subtle energy called chi or prana begins to relax and expand. It is the energy contraction within the inner subtle body that gives the feeling of being a localized self within and as a body. We're not talking about the *concept* of self now, we are talking about how its *feels* on a sensory level. When the inner subtle body relaxes, because the mind relaxes, we experience a feeling of expansiveness, greater clarity, and emotional well-being.

Understanding gives us insight but may have no effect on the feeling tone of inner experience. You might get it intellectually, but there's no positive improvement in how you feel. Hence, meditation may help in bringing your mind into a calm state, and that is a good thing because the rest follows organically.

Question: Could you explain a bit more regarding the analogy of the mirror representing our changeless Nature as Awareness?

Answer: Our perceiving and knowing nature is like a mirror. All our experiences are reflections that appear in that mirror. It cannot be blocked in any way because whatever the state of mind, emotion, feeling, or perception that is reflected in our mirror-like nature is fully known in the experience of the reflection. That is what the mirror does: it "knows" the reflections. All the reflections appear in the emptiness of the mirror, and the emptiness of the mirror is what knows the reflections. No reflection can block that mirroring capacity. There is nothing in the mirror that could be blocked because the mirror is completely empty of any changeable qualities. *It is the emptiness of the mirror that is its freedom and potential for infinite experiences.*

Someone might say, "Well, I lose this quality of being the mirror when a strong sense of *me* is present." It does seem that way. But if you notice closely, the experience of *me* is what's occurring in the mirror as the current reflection. So the mirror is working perfectly. The strong sense of *me* is what the mirror is knowing, as well as the sense of frustration of not being able to sense the empty nature of the mirror. These are both the current reflections that are occurring in the mirror of awareness.

So take a moment to notice any thought, the sense of *me* as identity, an emotion, a feeling, or a perception. Now notice if that experience was known in the mirror of your awareness. Did it appear in the mirror of your awareness? If so, try the same with many other appearances. Did any appearance, thought, feeling, or perception that you actually *experienced*, not appear in awareness? Even when we think we are in a state of distraction, the topic of distraction appeared in awareness. It was the current reflection that appeared in your perfect functioning awareness.

"Distraction" is only a label placed on a certain mental experience that appears in awareness.

Now instead of dividing the awareness experience into two parts—the *awareness of* and the *separate experience*, consider that awareness is itself appearing as the experience. For example, when you have a thought in awareness, consider that awareness is manifesting as the thought, like waves on the ocean. The ocean is manifesting as waves. The waves are not "happening" to the ocean, they are the ocean. Notice the same with your thoughts, emotions, feelings, sense of self, and perceptions. Experiences are not happening *to* awareness, experiences *are* awareness. It's a radically different way of seeing things, a nondual perspective.

Question: You mentioned the Tibetan tradition of Dzogchen, or the Great Perfection teachings. Could you explain a bit more regarding their most essential instructions for practice? I am not sure how I would put these teachings into practice.

Answer: The key instructions are quite easy once you know the main principles. The Great Perfection teachings show that our current observing awareness or consciousness is already enlightened and perfect. First, we have to differentiate this perfect awareness from other levels of the mind's functioning, like thinking and imagining. When recognized, this perfect awareness is called *rigpa* in Tibetan. Rigpa is the single most important term in the Great Perfection teachings. Rigpa is this "naked" or bare awareness that is just observing all experience occurring in the mind. The simple process of seeing with your eyes can occur with or without thoughts about what you see. Likewise, rigpa awareness experiences both mental and perceptual content without engaging in judging, labeling, or thinking about the experiential events. Just as an exercise, consider that rigpa is your sphere of awareness that fills the space of your head and that it is looking out of your eyes. You, as this sphere of pure consciousness, are looking out your eyes. Recognize that you are this empty observingness that is just there by default. Within this sphere of clear awareness, thoughts can appear and disappear like clouds in the space of the sky. But the space of the sky is not altered by the appearance of clouds or their absence. So we can differentiate the clear space of the sky from the clouds or weather that appear in it. We can also differentiate between the space of our clear observing awareness and our thoughts that appear in it. This is the first aspect of being introduced to the ever-present rigpa awareness as our own unchanging condition.

When you recognize this directly, you simply continue recognizing this essential nature of our awareness, this pure observing. You relax completely all efforts to grasp or resist experience. You just notice that this clear awareness is always present under all circumstances. When fully recognized in a totally relaxed condition, yet vividly alert, you will experience an open, clear state of peaceful and enjoyable presence. In this condition you continue throughout the day to integrate your natural presence within all activities and experiences. As time goes by, you spend more and more time in rigpa awareness rather than in thinking and imagining. Rigpa awareness becomes clearer and less personal as the sense of *me* also dissolves, like just another cloud in the clear sky of pure awareness. You are in touch with the here and now, and being so enhances your competence in all actions that you perform. These are the most essential aspects of Dzogchen practice. Dzogchen master Ponlop Rinpoche taught:

> Our mind is primordially in the state of Rigpa (Knowing Awareness). Whatever state of mind we go through, whether it is a very heavy experience of ignorance or a very outrageous emotion of anger, we have never moved from the state of Rigpa. Our mind has always been in the state of Rigpa, but we don't realize it all the time.

In other words, you practice leaving your awareness empty and clear to experience without intentionally filling it with mental content such as judging, evaluating, resisting, or grasping. Eventually you will no longer feel a separation between awareness and its field of experience. That is the non-dual state of realization.

Chapter Six

Nonduality and Quantum Physics

Another aspect of understanding who and what we are in the universe is offered in cutting-edge scientific research and its spin-offs. I have been particularly interested in the philosophical and spiritual implications of quantum physics in general. Many quantum physicists since the 1930s have taken the position that consciousness or awareness itself may not be a product of the brain; it may be part of the fabric of the universe itself at its most basic level, from the very beginning. I have spent many years studying this topic and have been curious regarding the close linkages between Eastern thought and quantum physics. From these studies I am convinced that there is a Quantum Intelligence that pervades and informs all phenomena on every level, whether subatomic or on the macro-level. It is also from understanding the quantum aspects of consciousness regarding extrasensory perception, telepathy, clairvoyance, and synchronicity that a more clear and scientific understanding of these phenomena is possible. I believe that it is this generic Quantum Intelligence that mystics and others have been tapping into for millennia and describing according to their own cultural and religious milieu. I also feel that a deeper level of consciousness, a Quantum Intelligence, was involved in my clairvoyant experience in Saudi Arabia, the Sufi clairvoyant in Kashmir, and the dream experience, all of which I shared in the first chapter.

Throughout my life I have noticed profound moments of synchronicity, which were often rather shocking moments of "coincidence." I remember one such occurrence when I was listening to an internet audio recording concerning higher states of awareness. I was also at the same time visually scanning a text I had recently written for any obvious typos. At the moment my eyes fell on the words in my text "Oh, my god," the speaker in the recording said "Oh, my god!" At first I thought how strange that those words I read sounded like the speaker's voice in the recording. But then I played the recording back and, sure enough, the speaker actually said "Oh, my god!" What are the odds that my eyes would fall on those words as the speaker was saying them at the exact same second? I thought "Oh my god, how strange!"

Stanislav Grof, the founder of transpersonal psychology, wrote:

> Most of us have encountered strange coincidences that defy ordinary explanation. The Austrian biologist Paul Kammerer, one of the first to be interested in the scientific implications of this phenomenon, reported a situation where his tram ticket bore the same number as the theater ticket that he bought immediately afterward; later that evening the same sequence of digits was given to him as a telephone number. The astronomer Flammarion cited an amusing story of a triple coincidence involving a certain Mr. Deschamps and a special kind of plum pudding. As a boy, Deschamps was given a piece of this pudding by a Mr. de Fortgibu. Ten years later, he saw the same pudding on the menu of a Paris restaurant and asked the waiter for a serving. However, it turned out that the last piece of the pudding was already ordered—by Mr. de Fortgibu, who just happened to be in the restaurant at that moment.

Many years later, Mr. Deschamps was invited to a party where this pudding was to be served as a special rarity. While he was eating it, he remarked that the only thing lacking was Mr. de Fortgibu. At that moment the door opened and an old man walked in. It was Mr. de Fortgibu who burst in on the party by mistake because he had been given a wrong address for the place he was supposed to go.

I consider such moments of synchronicity to be quantum events, moments when interdependent connections at a deep level of reality appear to surface consciousness. I never felt these events to be meaningless anomalies. Quite to the contrary, I always felt that this Quantum Intelligence was making its presence felt. I came away each time with a renewed sense of trust in this all-pervasive Universal Intelligence that seemed to express Itself in very mysterious yet meaningful ways. I believe that this Intelligence is currently communicating to us through the language of quantum physics. As we continue to learn more about the fabric and structure of the universe, consciousness itself is appearing to be an ever more important part of that research. Let's take a brief look at where current trends in quantum physics are heading.

To avoid getting bogged down in theory, I will discuss only those points that I feel are germane to consciousness and the mind. Let's first lay some groundwork. Our usual level of experience in our everyday world could be called the world of classical physics. Here everything follows the rules in an orderly process that is predictable and subject to the laws of cause and effect, gravity, motion, and electromagnetism, to name a few common elements of physics dating from the time of Sir Isaac Newton. In our dimension of experience, objects and energies have specific locations in space and time that are easily recognized. We could call this dimension the *macro world* as it relates to the bigger things that we can see with the naked eye and measure with conventional means. Then we can call the *micro world* of subatomic particles and their behaviors, the *quantum world*. The word *quantum* refers to super-small energy appearances, among the smallest possible, that seem to follow a different set of rules than classical physics suggests. Most but not all quantum phenomena appear in minute processes that occur at the size of atoms and considerably smaller scales of energy, outside the range of unaided human perception. However there are a few examples of quantum phenomena that are observable in our classical realm of experience, the most well known being the laser. Lasers function the way they do because quantum-level processes are involved regarding the way photons line up so orderly and maintain consistent and coherent beams of light. It is also possible that the human brain is itself a combination of two systems, a classical physics computer and a quantum computer. Let's explore a little bit regarding the latest findings in neuroscience and quantum physics on this topic.

Latest insights into brain research and quantum information processing offer new paradigms of reality. It is broadly accepted in quantum physics that the most elementary particle in the universe is not a material particle at all. It is a *bit* of information, and the universe is a vast field of information, as opposed to solid objects and energy particles. An observer receives the information as perceptions, processes them in the mind, then the information appears as sensory experience according to the information coded within the perceptual input. This view moves the universe one step closer to being pure consciousness because all materiality is reduced to *bits* of quantum information called *q-bits*. We could also call information knowledge or even wisdom. This also solves the enigma of how a material universe could arise from nothing. It didn't. What appeared from nothing was information. This is proven in quantum experiments on a regular basis, as subatomic "particles" appear spontaneously from nothing and then just as mysteriously disappear again. But it is not really a particle that appears, it is a *bit* of information.

As the great quantum physicist John Wheeler said, "Its from *bits*." Things— as "its"—appear from *bits* of information. Information requires some kind of processor, like a computer, to interpret the meaning, just like radio waves need a receiver in order to be decoded as music. That's where individual minds and brains enter the picture. For organisms, the brain is the radio that decodes information coming through the five senses. We get not only sound but an entire hologram-like visual gestalt called the "universe", as produced by our mind. A theory of the nature of the universe that's been around for a few decades now is called the holographic model. Quantum physicist David Bohm, a close colleague of Albert Einstein's, was one of the earliest to speak of a holographic model of the universe in his 1980 book *Wholeness and the Implicate Order*.

Early on in the history of quantum physics, Albert Einstein and others noticed a very unusual phenomena: that if two sub-atomic particles, electrons for example, at some point had contact with each other and then separated; they would act as identical twins. If you separated the two electrons by a large distance, let's say millions of light years, and you then modified one of the twins; the other would manifest the change at the *exact* same moment. No time would elapse between the change in one and the change in the other. Somehow information was getting to the twin about the change *instantly*. This actually turned out to be a problem for Einstein; further testing later confirmed that the information would have to travel faster than the speed of light, and Einstein had said the speed limit for the universe was set at the speed of light. How could this be?

Many physicists postulated various theories and one of the most interesting was presented by David Bohm. David Bohm's answer to that question was that reality was the visible unfolding of a deeply interior source that revealed itself as the world of classical physics, our world of experience—space, time, and objects.

Because everything unfolded from the same source, the information regarding how particles should appear or act was known in all places simultaneously. The entire universe is embedded within this Quantum Intelligence, which Bohm called the *implicate order*, which unfolds itself in what he called the *explicate order*. Basically in this sense, *implicate* means "inside," and *explicate* means "outer apparent." But things also go in reverse; they can disappear and enfold back into the source.

A good example of this is our thoughts. A thought appears out of the mind or source, then disappears, but can reappear later. Bohm felt that all things are an inseparable oneness and facets of a single common ground. What is known *here* can be known *there* at the same time. He referred to this common ground of all existence as the *holomovement*. The universe functions as a giant hologram wherein the entirety is enfolded into each individual appearance. This model could account for telepathy and other extrasensory phenomena, and it solves the quantum enigma that puzzled Einstein until his dying day. It could be that telepathy is not about one person knowing what's in another's mind. Rather, there is only one mind, and the idea of two separate persons is just an illusion. This is like Bohm's point that there are not two particles acting like "identical twins," but in fact there was always only one particle.

I have spent a lot of time researching the latest views in quantum physics and brain neuroscience regarding the theory that the universe is indeed one vast hologram that includes our body, brain, thoughts, and sense of self. I have been interested in this theory since I first read about it in the early 1980s. I sensed it was true but needed more scientific support. Today that support for the holographic model of the universe is becoming ever more solid.

Einstein felt his successor would likely be his protégé, Bohm, who was one of the first to have established a coherent theory that the universe is a hologram. Further research in quantum physics supports his theory, especially most recently, which clarifies hitherto unexplained phenomena regarding the physical and quantum worlds quite satisfactorily.

Along with this, one of the world's most distinguished brain scientists, Karl Pribram, proposed in the 1960s that the brain functioned holographically. Through his vigorous research, he found that unresolved issues concerning memory storage and other brain functions could be resolved when incorporated into a model of the brain operating holographically. This position has gained growing and continuing support within the scientific community. Pribram and Bohm eventually got together and compared notes. They concluded that the entire universe is fully holographic, including us. That means our brains are also holograms along with our bodies.

Today there are many quantum physicists, philosophers, neuroscientists, and brain researchers who are intrigued by the idea that many of the aspects of quantum physics may apply to human consciousness. The similarities between the two worlds of quantum physics and research in human consciousness are nothing less than amazing. From the earliest days of quantum physics there have been discussions that human consciousness may be a necessary component for a complete understanding of how quantum processes operate in our world of experience. In some quantum experiments, it seems an observer affects the results of the experiment. The mere presence of an observer or measuring device affects the experiments out come. So our experience of reality is not just dependent on what is observed but also on the nature of the observer. This leads to further questions regarding the mysterious nature of consciousness, the mind, and the brain.

Dr. Pribram wrote an article that mentioned a bit about extrasensory perception (ESP) and other interesting topics related to the model of the holographic brain. He thought mystics and others may have been discovering the holographic nature of the universe for thousands of years, especially in Buddhist and Hindu descriptions of the universe. But Kabbalah, Sufism, and Eastern Orthodox Christianity also espouse similar models.

Pribram wrote in 1968:

> Scientists are, as yet, only barely acquainted with the implicate holographic order. I believe, however, that it is this order which is being explored experientially by mystics, psychics and others delving in paranormal phenomena. Perhaps if the rules for "tuning-in" on the holographic implicate domain could be made more explicit we could attain that scientific understanding of paranormal phenomena that we aim for in conferences such as this. As set out in the introduction, true scientific sharing depends on this base of understanding, not just on proving the reliability of experimental realities. I believe that the paradigm shift in science, occasioned by the' insights obtained in quantum physics and carried forward by the holographic model of brain function, will, in fact, provide us with that base of understanding which makes it clear that the world of appearances is but a reciprocal of another reality, a reality that may already have been explored experientially for untold millennia.

My second book, *The Way of Light*, will document in great detail the teachings and practices of traditions centered around realizing our true nature to be a most ineffable and changeless Clear Light Awareness. These traditions describe the universe as an expression of that Light. Modulations of Light frequencies intersect everywhere and appear as a vast hologram floating in the empty space of pure Awareness. We are that empty space of pure Awareness, and our creativity appears as infinite displays of holographic dimensions of color, light and sound that are no different than images appearing in a mirror.

In ancient Hua Yen Buddhism there is a description of reality similar to the notion of a holographic universe. It says that everything is contained within every other individual part. This interconnected web of relationships is known as the Net of Indra. Indra is one of the highest Hindu gods.

In his book The Enlightened Mind, Stephen Mitchell wrote:

> The Net of Indra is a profound and subtle metaphor for the structure of reality. Imagine a vast net; at each crossing point there is a jewel; each jewel is perfectly clear and reflects all the other jewels in the net, the way two mirrors placed opposite each other will reflect an image ad infinitum. The jewel in this metaphor stands for an individual being, or an individual consciousness, or a cell or an atom. Every jewel is intimately connected with all other jewels in the universe, and a change in one jewel means a change, however slight, in every other jewel.

Eventually Bohm confided in Pribram that he felt the universe itself was only "thought." Today's quantum physics is becoming comfortable with the notion that consciousness has a role in shaping our experience. For us the universe doesn't take form until its *information* is observed, processed, and generated as the 3-D experience that occurs in our brain. Some prominent quantum physicists such as Brian Greene and Leonard Susskind believe the universe is essentially two-dimensional information that then is projected as a 3-D hologram. Once that two-dimensional information is processed through consciousness or the brain, it appears as a three-dimensional hologram. In other words, the universe, including your body and brain, is a giant hologram. That fits in with Pribram's work demonstrating that the brain functions holographically. It is the nature of a hologram that any single part of it contains the entire hologram. So you could say the entire universe is in your big toe, or little toe, for that matter. That is not exaggerating. It means that any thought contains the whole universe because everything is part of the hologram, and the entire universe is encoded within every single part.

This concept of the entire universe being enfolded within even the smallest part has been shared by poets and mystics alike. William Blake wrote:

> To see a world in a grain of sand,
>
> And a heaven in a wild flower,
>
> Hold infinity in the palm of your hand,
>
> And eternity in an hour.

Brian Greene, professor of physics and of mathematics at Columbia University, is widely regarded for a number of ground-breaking discoveries in superstring theory. In his book *The Elegant Universe: Superstrings, Hidden Dimensions, and the Quest for an Ultimate Theory,* he wrote:

> Physics and everything we know in the world around us may really be tied to processes whose fundamental existence is not here around us, but rather exists in some distant bounding surface like some thin hologram, which by virtue of illuminating it in the right way can reproduce what looks like a 3-dimensional world. Perhaps our three dimensional world is really just a holographic illumination of laws that exist on some thin bounding slice, like that thin little piece of plastic, that thin hologram. It's an amazing idea, and I think

is likely to be where physics goes in the next few years or in the next decade, at least when one's talking about quantum gravity or quantum string theory.

Bohm's view as expressed below is in keeping with today's latest cutting-edge insights into the nature of the universe as understood in quantum physics. In the emerging view, the entire universe is just *information*, not "energy." The universe only has meaning and structure when "decoded" by a conscious mind. Bohm wrote:

> The tangible reality of our everyday lives is really a kind of illusion, like a holographic image. Underlying it is a deeper order of existence, a vast and more primary level of reality that gives birth to all the objects and appearances of our physical world in much the same way that a piece of holographic film gives birth to a hologram. If the concreteness of the world is but a secondary reality, and what is "out there" is actually a holographic blur of frequencies, and if the brain is also a hologram and only processes some of the frequencies out of this blur, what becomes of objective reality? Put quite simply, it ceases to exist. Although we may think we are physical beings moving through a physical world, this is an illusion. We are really "receivers" floating through a kaleidoscopic sea of frequency.

In his book *Decoding Reality: The Universe as Quantum Information*, Vlatko Vedral currently professor of Quantum Information Theory at Oxford, England wrote about several aspects of quantum information theory that tie in nicely with Bohm's ideas. Vedral reduces the universe to its basic building blocks of q-bits of information. Here are some key quotes from his book:

Unsurprisingly, the language Nature uses to communicate is "information"...

Eastern religion and philosophy have a strong core of relational thinking...What emptiness means in Buddhism is that "things" do not exist in themselves, but are only possible in relation to other "things"...

It might seem desirable to distinguish the "mathematical fictions" from "actual particles"; but it is difficult to find any logical basis for such a distinction. Discovering a particle means observing certain effects which are accepted as proof of its existence. [British Astronomer Arthur Stanley] Eddington claims here that a particle is just a set of labels that we use to describe outcomes of our measurements. And that's it...

It all boils down to a relation between our measurements and our labels! The complexity that we see around us in this world (and this complexity we believe to be growing with time, as far as life is concerned at least) is just due to the growing interconnectedness. In this way, can we now analyse how we encode reality? By doing so, we will never arrive at 'the thing in itself' by any kind of means. Everything that exists, exists by convention and labelling and is therefore dependent on other things. So, Buddhists would say that their highest goal—realizing emptiness—simply means that we realize how inter-related things fundamentally are...

We have reached a point where any particle of matter (such as an atom) and energy (such as a photon) in the Universe is defined with respect to an intricate procedure that is used to detect it. If the detector makes a click (like a Geiger counter) the particle is detected. The click itself creates one extra bit of information comprising reality. The crucial point is that the particle does not exist independently of the detector.

The click has no cause at all and therefore we have no underlying particles. And since there are no underlying particles in reality, there are no things in the Universe that are made up of particles existing without the intricate procedures to detect them...

Anything that exists in this Universe, anything to which you can attribute any kind of reality, only exists by virtue of the mutual information it shares with other objects in the Universe. Underneath this, nothing else exists, nothing else has any underlying reality...

It is counterintuitive that although we seem to perceive a well-defined reality around us, quantum physics suggests that there is no underlying single reality in the Universe independent of us—and that our reality is actually only defined if and when we observe it...

The Universe starts empty but potentially with a huge amount of information. The key event that gives the Universe some direction is the first act of "symmetry breaking," the first cut of the sculptor. This act, which we consider as completely random, i.e., without any prior cause, just decides on why one tiny aspect in the Universe is one way rather than another...

But where do these qubits (bits of information as the basis of the universe) come from? Quantum theory allows us to answer this question; but the answer is not quite what we expected. It suggests that these qubits come from nowhere! There is no prior information required in order for information to exist. Information can be created from emptiness...

Within our reality everything exists through an interconnected web of relationships and the building blocks of this web are bits of information. We process, synthesize, and observe this information in order to construct the reality around us. As information spontaneously emerges from the emptiness we take this into account to update our view of reality. The laws of Nature are information about information and outside of it there is just darkness. This is the gateway to understanding reality. And I finish with a quote from the Tao Te Ching, which some 2500 years earlier, seems to have beaten me to the punch-line: The Tao that can be told is not the eternal Tao. The name that can be named is not the eternal name. The nameless is the beginning of heaven and earth. The named is the mother of the ten thousand things. Ever desireless, one can see the mystery. Ever desiring, one sees the manifestations. These two spring from the same source but differ in name; this appears as darkness. Darkness within darkness. The gate to all mystery.

For humans, our brains do an amazing job of interpretation of incoming information. However, our brain and mind function as two integrated computer operating systems. One operates along the lines of classical physics, in which stimulus-response and organism survival computations are dominant, and the other operates more along the lines of a quantum computer, in which pure reason, intuition, imagination, extrasensory perception, and spiritual insights are possible. The classical brain processes sensory information and distributes the information cognitively to consciousness in packets or chunks called thoughts. However, the quantum mind can receive higher wavelengths of information and distributes this knowledge through a much faster and "cleaner" method experienced as insights or intuitions. I say cleaner because the quantum processing bypasses the various stimulus response associative aspects of discursive thought and conditioning.

As the capacity of the quantum mind is further enhanced, one may experience a much more intuitive functioning along the lines of extrasensory perceptions such as telepathy, clairvoyance, and observations of unexplainable synchronicity. Omniscience is simply the ability to decode information that makes up everything in the universe. A moment of enlightenment is a sudden ability to see or read the overall information blueprint for the entirety of reality regarding consciousness and being. These quantum super-insights appear from the nothingness or emptiness from which all information arises spontaneously. This space could be called the quantum space of "superposition," the yet not actualized dimension of infinite possibility. This superposition state is also known as the non-local wave state. When the non-localized wave state of light "collapses" due to being observed or measured, it appears as a localized "particle" or photon in space and time. So light can appear as a particle or as a wave. Our individual consciousness appears to have the same characteristics, as we will discuss further below.

The quantum information regarding enlightenment exists independently of the database of our classical stimulus-response brain. Yet the mind-blowing quantum enlightenment information will still be downloaded but only in a limited form as the capacity to process and store such quantum information is not possible by the brain. Quantum enlightenment only exists in quantum "super-position" as the wave state of consciousness. That's why individuals who have had this enlightenment experience say it is impossible to put it into words.

It would seem a worthy task to access or enhance our quantum mind as much as possible rather than remain with the highly limited and task-focused perspectives of our brains. To accomplish this we need to differentiate the two systems used for all our information processing. Normal thinking and conceptualizing are the everyday functioning of the classical brain. Non-conceptual awareness and cognitive insights are the most prominent functions of the quantum mind. By taking the position of residing in non-conceptual awareness, we observe the operations of the classical brain as they arise. We notice an endless stream of thoughts, images, and their stories. We also notice a sense of self-identity as a subjective self within various stories. This sense of personal self is strictly a construction of stimulus-response conditioning within the classical computer. This mind takes its information and turns it into concrete, separate subjects and objects holographically. That's why our world seems so solid and enduring, even though physics has shown it is not solid at all but mostly space.

Our usual way of experiencing the world is purely an interpretation based on the parameters of our hardware and software settings as determined by DNA and conditioning. We know insects, for example, have a different sensory interpretation of the same information that we experience. In our experience a data stream of information is coming in and is processed in a very subjective way. No perceiver is perceiving a static objective world that exists as perceived. We are only experiencing what our hardware and software interprets and projects. The mind interprets perceptual experiences based on its software database of prior experience, which adds an evaluative nuance to otherwise completely neutral events. This is how the mind creates its own heaven and hell from neutral experience. By deactivating the mind's automaticity of believing in its own assessments, opinions, and evaluations as being the "truth of reality," we find a relaxed and appreciative state of consciousness. But in order to do this we need to bring the quantum mind into play to override the old hardware and software programs of the conditioned mind.

Further support that consciousness itself and thought processes may also be occurring on the quantum level exists according to several interesting studies done over the last fifty years. It may be, as mentioned above, that the brain is a combination of a classical bio-computer and a quantum processor of information feeding from two separate sources. The brain relates to sensory perceptions and physical experiences, and the quantum system deals with memory, creative thought, awareness, consciousness, imagination, dreaming, mystical experience, enlightenment, extra-sensory phenomena like telepathy, clairvoyance, synchronicity, out-of-body experience, near-death experiences, and other unusual aspects of consciousness. Some scientists have suggested that there may be a quantum level of functioning within the brain cells themselves. However, it may be that consciousness and awareness are themselves independent of the brain and exist within a dimension that I call Quantum Intelligence, an all-pervasive field that permeates energy and space as the Ground of Being. The research on this is extremely interesting, and you can review some of the work done by Stuart Hameroff, Karl Pribram, Roger Penrose, David Bohm, and Amit Goswami, among many others.

Whereas neuroscientists are focusing on the brain in order to understand the quantum mind, you can directly access it through working with inner energy centers called chakras, as described in chapter 5. For example, by activating the crown chakra inside the skull, you can access higher states of quantum consciousness. When you open and activate the third-eye chakra located between the eyes just above the bridge of the nose, you can experience other quantum dimensions of reality. It seems we are able to gain access into David Bohm's *Implicate Order,* the very heart of the cosmic hologram, with these and other inner light body practices.

Energy can exist at our level of experience, the level of classical physics, or as potential that has not yet entered the dimension of *things* in space and time. For example, as previously mentioned, when you observe light, it can appear as a wave, the exact position of which can't be measured. It has no apparent substance that can be localized. Or light can appear as a photon, a particle that can be measured and has a specific location in space and time, but only when measured. In quantum physics, subatomic particles follow the same principles. The particles don't actually exist in space and time until someone observes them or attempts to measure their position or velocity. They are only a mathematical probability. Once observed, the wave state of a quantum potential "collapses" and a subatomic "particle" now appears in our dimension of classical physics. Before the collapse, the particle had no actual existence; it was only a potential or probability.

We could similarly say that matter and energy remain in the mind of God, or "super-position," until they are brought into the dimension of created things. Until a conscious observer participates, nothing appears and takes form from the dimension of pure potential. We can use the analogy of an artist. He has his artistic image in mind, but until he lifts his brush and begins to paint, his painting only exists as potential in his mind. Expression of reality is likewise extremely creative because there's no set rule of what and how things should be manifesting. It's all fluid in coordination with the nature, perspective, and timing of the observing consciousness.

Let's apply quantum theory to our experience. What if our sense of being an individual, our personal self-identity, is the result of one of these quantum collapses? Consciousness as Quantum Intelligence exists as itself only as an undefined quantum state of potential. Being consciousness itself, it is in a state of being that is undifferentiated. It is everywhere because Quantum Intelligence is present at the absolute smallest possible space as the ground in which everything is embedded, perhaps at the level of what is called the Planck Scale. Let's say that this Quantum Intelligence reflects on itself through consciousness, like dreaming. In other words, it observes itself just as the quantum physicist "observes" quantum phenomena. At that moment of observation, the quantum wave collapses into our dimension of space and time as a "unit" or particle. Similarly, I suggest that when Quantum Intelligence reflects on itself through thought, there is an immediate collapse of consciousness into the dimension of space and time appearing as a "unit" of consciousness. That would be the birth of an apparent self. It has location and definition in consciousness. It's our individual viewpoint. It's a collapsed state of consciousness now appearing as an assumed viewpoint in space and time. The empty, space-like awareness as the pure Ground of Being doesn't collapse, only its dimension or energy field of creative consciousness collapses. It collapses around the pure Ground of Being like a contracted sphere with a pure and aware empty center. The quality of pure awareness in the middle remains unchanged, just like the clear glass of a mirror remains untouched by the reflections within it.

However, the collapse can be reversed. That which brought about the collapse can also be used in principle to precipitate a return to the original Quantum Intelligence state. Remember, *self*-consciousness created the collapse, so that would mean that by the individual becoming "un-*self*-conscious," the original state could be regained. The more we focus on ourselves as a separate "me," the longer experience remains in the collapsed condition. The collapsed condition is a state of mind resulting from the mind's fundamental ignorance; a *not knowing* of our perfect, *wave-state* primordial nature. This "not knowing" is the cause of our suffering.

Hasn't this always been the message of the masters and the mystics? By freeing ourselves of our narcissistic self-conscious fixations, we shift into the Ground of Being, the undefined state of Quantum Intelligence. This moment is called enlightenment.

From this shift we experience consciousness beyond limitations of self, time, and space. Further, the inherent qualities of bliss, love, peace, and profound wisdom blossom freely. These are all intrinsic qualities of Quantum Intelligence.

Finally, I would like to discuss the quantum phenomenon of advanced spiritual development that is part of many esoteric traditions. This phenomenon is most well known in Tibetan culture from ancient times, and such occurrences are still reported. Here is a report by the Dalai Lama regarding this phenomenon:

> Two years ago a Tibetan yogi who practiced the Great Perfection, Dzogchen, style of meditation in the Nyingma tradition achieved a state of the complete disappearance of his gross physical body, which we call "achieving a rainbow body." His name was Achok, and he was from Nyarong. He studied philosophy from time to time at a Geluk monastic university near Lhasa called Sera, and he also received teachings from my junior tutor Trijang Rinpochay, but his main teacher was the Nyingma lama, Dujom Rinpochay. Although he practiced Tantra according to both the old and new schools of Tibetan Buddhism, his main practice was the recitation of "om mani padme hum" and its accompanying meditation.

> Until about three years ago, he frequently said he hoped to have the opportunity of meeting the Dalai Lama in this lifetime. Then, one day he called on his followers to perform offerings for the sake of the Dalai Lama's life. After they made offerings, he surprised them by announcing that he would leave. He put on his saffron monastic robe and told them to seal him inside his room for a week. His disciples followed his request and after a week opened the room to find that he had completely

disappeared except for his robe. One of his disciples and a fellow practitioner came to Dharmsala, where they related the story to me and gave me a piece of his robe.

Since he usually remained in retreat as a very simple monk with no pretensions, unlike some lamas, he proved that he was a good practitioner and finally this occurred. You can see the connection between cause and effect. There are others about whom miracles are claimed, but without the proper causes...

Our aim is to manifest the fundamental innate mind of clear light, the most subtle level of consciousness, and to remain within that level of mind without regressing to grosser levels. However, this purified state is not just mental; it involves body, but a body fashioned from prana, the prana that is the mount of the mind of clear light. The ultimate purpose of these manifestations is to assist others in achieving the same freedom from suffering and limitation.

The center of this process of purification is realization of the luminous and knowing nature of mind—understanding that afflictive emotions such as lust, hatred, enmity, jealousy, and belligerence do not reside in the very essence of mind but are peripheral to it. When the mind knows its own nature and when this knowledge is teamed with powerful concentration, it gradually becomes possible to reduce and finally to overcome the afflictive states that drive the process of repeated suffering. This is the Tibetan view of the intimate relationship between mind and matter, and how they work in the process of altruistically directed purification. (From *Mind of Clear Light: Advice on Living Well and Dying Consciously by His Holiness the Dalai Lama*, translated and edited by Jeffrey Hopkins.)

Here is another very interesting article on the same topic of the "Body of Light" transformations. It further confirms the report of the Dalai Lama concerning the same lama:

> When David Steindl-Rast, a Benedictine monk, pro-posed investigating the "rainbow body," a phenome-non in which the corpses of highly developed spiritual individuals reputedly vanish within days of death, he received an enthusiastic response from Marilyn Schlitz, IONS's director of research.

> In a new joint initiative with the Esalen Institute, IONS is expanding its research on "metanormal capaci-ties"—behaviors, experiences, and bodily changes that challenge our understanding of ordinary human func-tioning—because they raise crucial questions about the developmental potential of human beings.

> "Brother David told us that he had taken this project to various institutions and foundations looking for sup-port," recalls Schlitz. His intention was to corroborate these claims, and accumulate data that would not only help us understand more about the rainbow body, but also look at its broader implications. He had been told that this type of research is unacceptable within main-stream science. But, I said, "This is exactly the kind of project we're interested in at IONS. As long as the research can be conceptualized within a rigorous critical frame, we are open to examining any and all questions that can expand our idea of what is possible as humans."

> Steindl-Rast's own curiosity about the rainbow body began when he heard various stories of Tibetan masters who had, through their practices, reached a high degree of wisdom and compassion. It was reported to him that when they died, rainbows suddenly appeared in the

sky. "And I was told that after several days their bodies disappeared. Sometimes fingernails and hair were left. Sometimes nothing was left."

These stories made him reflect upon the resurrection of Jesus Christ, which is central to his own faith. "We know that Jesus was a very compassionate, selfless person. When he died, according to the gospels, his body was no longer there."

In today's world, Steindl-Rast points out, the resurrection of Jesus Christ is interpreted differently, depending upon one's spiritual leanings. For fundamentalists, the resurrection—the act of rising from the dead—happened only to Jesus, and couldn't happen to any other human. The minimalists, on the other hand, says Steindl-Rast, focus on Jesus's spirit living on, and believe that the resurrection of Jesus had nothing to do with his body.

Yet, a large number of people (including himself) are open to the concept that the body, too, is significant in the spiritual realm, and that certain spiritual experiences are universal.

In 1999, he decided to explore the strange phenomenon of the rainbow body and a possible connection to the resurrection of Jesus. "I sent a fax to a friend in Switzerland, who is a Zen Buddhist teacher. I knew that many Tibetans live there, and so I asked him if he could inquire about the rainbow body. Two days later, I received a fax back stating that a Tibetan had unexpectedly approached him, and when the rainbow body was mentioned, the Tibetan said, 'It happened to one of my teachers just recently, and a famous lama who witnessed the events wrote an account about them.'" At this point, Steindl-Rast contacted Father Francis Tiso, an ordained Roman Catholic priest who has not only studied ten languages, including Tibetan, but is also familiar with Tibetan culture. (Francis Tiso holds the office of Canon in the Cathedral of St Peter, Isernia, Italy, and is assigned to the Archdiocese of San Francisco, where he is parochial vicar in Mill Valley.)

"I was aware," says Steindl-Rast, "that Father Tiso occasionally went to Tibet, so I asked him if he was planning to travel there in the near future. He told me he was leaving that very day."

Steindl-Rast asked if he would stop in Switzerland and interview the Tibetan. Despite the short notice, Tiso took a detour to Switzerland, and thus the research journey began.

The rainbow body is a complex phenomenon that will probably take years of study. "If we can establish as an anthropological fact," says Steindl-Rast, "that what is described in the resurrection of Jesus has not only happened to others, but is happening today, it would put our view of human potential in a completely different light."

Recent Rainbow Body Experiences

Through his Swiss contact, Tiso received the name of the monk whose body had vanished after his death: Khenpo A-chos, a Gelugpa monk from Kham, Tibet, who died in 1998. Tiso was able to locate the village, situated in a remote area where Khenpo A-chos had his hermitage. He then went to the village and conducted taped interviews with eyewitnesses to Khenpo A-chos' death. He also spoke to many people who had known him.

"This was a very interesting man, aside from the way he died," observes Tiso. "Everyone mentioned his faithfulness to his vows, his purity of life, and how he often spoke of the importance of cultivating compassion. He had the ability to teach even the roughest and toughest of types how to be a little gentler, a little more mindful. To be in the man's presence changed people."

Tiso interviewed Lama Norta, a nephew of Khenpo Achos; Lama Sonam Gyamtso, a young disciple; and Lama A-chos, a dharma friend of the late Khenpo A-chos. They described the following:

A few days before Khenpo A-chos died, a rainbow appeared directly above his hut. After he died, there were dozens of rainbows in the sky. Khenpo A-chos died lying on his right side. He wasn't sick; there appeared to be nothing wrong with him, and he was reciting the mantra OM MANI PADME HUM over and over. According to the eyewitnesses, after his breath stopped his flesh became kind of pinkish. One person said it turned brilliant white. All said it started to shine.

Lama A-chos suggested wrapping his friend's body in a yellow robe, the type all Gelug monks wear. As the days passed, they maintained they could see, through the robe, that his bones and his body were shrinking. They also heard beautiful, mysterious music coming from the sky, and they smelled perfume.

After seven days, they removed the yellow cloth, and no body remained. Lama Norta and a few other individuals claimed that after his death Khenpo A-chos appeared to them in visions and dreams.

Other Rainbow Body Manifestations

Francis Tiso remarks that one of his most intriguing interviews was with Lama A-chos. He told Tiso that when he died he too would manifest the rainbow body. "He showed us two photographs taken of him in the dark, and in these photographs his body radiated rays of light."

Because Lama A-chos emphasized that it was possible to manifest the rainbow body while still alive, not just in death, Tiso plans to return to Tibet with professional camera equipment to try to photograph this radiating light.

Other incidents of metanormal occurrences upon death are also being studied. For instance, several of Tiso's colleagues were present for the postmortem process of Dilgo Khyentse Rinpoche, who died eight years ago. "This man was a very large-boned individual," says Tiso, "and it was reported that seven weeks after his death the flesh was reduced. That could have been done by chemical substances, however, the bones also shrank."

Shrinkage of the body occurred with another guru, Lama Thubten. His miniature-sized frame is now kept in a monastery in Manali, India. Tiso has ascertained that incidents of bodies shrinking or disappearing shortly after death were documented centuries ago, such as in the classic story of Milarepa, a Buddhist saint from Tibet who lived in the 11th century. Milarepa's biography was translated into French by Jacques Bacot in 1912, and into English by Walter Evans-Wentz in the 1920s.

"In the ninth chapter of this literary classic," explains Tiso, who wrote a dissertation about the Buddhist saint,

"It states that his body completely disappeared shortly after his death."

Even the earliest biographies of Milarepa, says Tiso, attest to this phenomenon. In addition, accounts exist about the great eighth-century tantric master Padma-sambhava and how his body vanished.

The Significance of Practice and Culture

When conducting this type of research, says Tiso, it is important not only to interview as many people as possible, but also to study biographies and any written explanations of these events. When he arrived in Tibet to investigate the death of Khenpo A-chos, Tiso was fortunate enough to obtain the bulk of his biography by Sonam Phuntsok within an hour of his arrival.

What is at stake, explains Tiso, is not simply verification of a phenomenon, but understanding the values, spiritual practices, and culture in which this phenomenon is embedded. "We need to examine these institutions and practices in a new light in order to recover for humanity some very profound truths about the expansion of the human consciousness and our potential as human beings."

This opportunity is present in the Nyarong region in Tibet, where several incidences of the rainbow body are said to have occurred. The research team is now studying their way of life, especially their spiritual practices.

Tiso has also obtained copies of spiritual retreat manuals, which have been particularly helpful.

Lama A-chos told Tiso that it takes sixty years of intensive practice to achieve the rainbow body. "Whether it always takes that long, I don't know," acknowledges Tiso, "but we would like to be able to incorporate, in a respectful way, some of these practices into our own Western philosophical and religious traditions."

At the same time, continues Tiso, the research team plans to expend the scope of this research beyond the confines of the Tibetan culture, so they can compare the rainbow body phenomenon with the resurrection of Jesus Christ. To our knowledge, says Tiso, the bodies of most Christian saints did not disappear or shrink after their deaths.

"Highly realized saints in Catholic and Orthodox Christianity tend to move in the direction of incorruption, so that the body does not decay after death."

However, he adds, bodily ascensions are mentioned in the Bible and other traditional texts for Enoch, Mary, Elijah, and possibly Moses. And there are numerous stories of saints materializing after their death, similar to the widespread phenomenon known as the "light-body."

"In my church of Saints Cosmas and Damian in Italy, we have a large number of accounts, going back centuries, that indicate that these saints appeared in dreams and visions, rescued people from harm, and cured them of diseases. Even today, people still tell me they have these visions," says Tiso.

In 1984, when Tiso was meditating with his eyes open in a chapel in Italy, he, too, had an extraordinary vision. Jesus Christ, he says, appeared before him in the form of a violet light-body. At that time, Tiso was considering taking a teaching position in the United States, but in this vision Christ indicated he should stay in Italy. "It was important not to make a mistake at that point in my life," reflects Tiso. "I did stay in Italy, where I was eventually ordained, and I lived in a hermitage chapel for almost twelve years."

Tiso has also had several Tibetan teachers appear to him in dreams. When he gives public lectures he speaks frankly about these experiences, because he feels it is important for people to understand that they are more common than we think. "I think that as people mature in their spiritual practice, they begin to have visionary experiences."

Recent Implications

Countries such as China, Tiso notes, and certain political movements in Western Europe have chosen to abandon and even physically destroy anything to do with the contemplative life. "We're now being asked to examine those institutions and their practices in a new light in order to recover for humanity some very profound truths about who we are as human beings."

This research is clearly controversial because it tackles the age-old questions of life after death, the immortal soul, and reincarnation. Furthermore, it suggests that the alleged resurrection of Jesus Christ was not an isolated case, but shines as an example of what may be possible for all human beings.

Both Tiso and Steindl-Rast emphasize that these experiences are said to occur only in highly evolved individuals who are the embodiment of compassion and love. They speculate these qualities—conscience and consciousness—are a driving force of evolution. "It is my great hope that the rainbow body research will make us more aware of this possibility," says Steindl-Rast.

Tiso holds the opinion that in today's world, where consumerism, exploitation, and economic injustice are still out of control, there is an urgent need to reinforce the more loving, altruistic, and spiritual dimensions of the human being. In the future, he says, we should consider establishing new models of monasteries and retreat centers for individuals who wish, with idealistic motivations, to intensify their spiritual practices. He also proposes initiating a "holy" laboratory to document the progress of individuals.

As for the rainbow body, Tiso and his team hope actually witness and scientifically document the entire experience while it is occurring.

"What is important" says Schlitz, "is that we broaden our scope of what we believe is possible. We want to discover if there are ways we can begin to develop spiritual practices that, even though they might not lead us to personally experience the rainbow body, could lead us to some other manifestation of our highest potential."

Gail Bernice Holland is an associate editor of IONS Review, and former editor of Connections. She is the author of A Call for Connection: Solutions for Creating a Whole New Culture (New World Library, 1998). Contact: gbauthor@noetic.org.

Brother David Steindl-Rast is the director of the Network For Grateful Living and oversees the content development of its website www.gratefulness.org

The phenomenon of the body disappearing through spiritual practice has occurred several times in the twentieth century. It is well documented in Tibet. These exact types of occurrences have occurred in other locations and cultures too. Probably the most famous was the vanishing of Christ's body after his crucifixion. Before his death, he also displayed his quantum "light body" in the Transfiguration on Mount Tabor to several witnesses as reported in the New Testament. Also, in the Greek Orthodox tradition there are many stories about saints living as hermits on the island of Mount Athos in Greece. A recurring theme occurs again and again for over the last several hundreds of years regarding the saintly hermits being seen either completely enshrouded in light or transformed into light. They say this light body tradition goes back to the time of Christ.

This poem by St. Symeon the New Theologian is from the tenth century:

How is it that you have clothed me

in the brilliant garment,

radiant with the splendor of immortality,

that turns all my members into light?

Your body, immaculate and divine,

is all radiant with the fire of your divinity...

with which it is ineffably joined and combined.

This is the gift you have given me, my God:

that this mortal and shabby frame

has become one with your immaculate body

that I have been made one with your divinity

and have become your own most pure body,

a brilliant member, transparently lucid,

luminous and holy.

I see the beauty of it all, I can gaze on the radiance.

I have become a reflection of the light of your grace.

When I was in Israel a few years ago, I had a rare opportunity to interview Rabbi Yitzchak Ginsburgh regarding several esoteric topics of the ancient Jewish mysticism called Kabbalah. The rabbi is one of its leading masters. We discussed the phenomena of the gradual disappearance of the physical body regarding masters of Kabbalah. He told me that he witnessed these phenomena regarding his teacher several years before. But in this case, it was not associated with the teacher's death but the gradual transparency of his body while still alive and functioning in the world. He explained that we have an inner "light body" of Divine Light. When we attain a high level of purification from negative thoughts and energies, the physical body is transformed by the degree of inner purity of heart. The body becomes pure Light.

The light body is called *tselem* in Hebrew, meaning "the image of God as created in the soul of man." Here's a quote from the fifteenth century by the Kabbalah master Rabbi Moses Isserles of Cracow:

> For in truth, it is fitting to describe Him by this parable and metaphor, for light is found with Him, on Him all those who gaze see, and each one sees in Him like one gazing in a mirror. For the *coarse matter* that is in man stands opposite...the one who contemplates, behind the clear light that is in the soul, which I liken to a mirror for him, and

he sees in it, in an inner vision, his own form. For this reason the prophets compared the divine glory (Kavod) to a human image, for they saw their own form. But Moses our teacher, because he had *removed from himself all corporeality and there is none of the dark matter from without, left within him saw naught but the brilliant Light itself,* and there was no (reflected) image, but he saw only the clear aspect.

Several of my Sufi teacher's disciples told me when I was in Kashmir that this same type of phenomenon occurred with our teacher, Qassim. They recounted a time they were gathered for a Sufi meeting on a small houseboat moored near the shoreline. There was a narrow plank of wood that was used as a short bridge to the shore. They had been in the meeting for several hours, during which it had been snowing heavily. They reported that Qassim said that he was going outside for a bit. Time went by and finally they decided to see where Qassim was. When they went outside, they found no footprints in the snow, neither on the boat nor on the shore. They could find no trace of Qassim. They returned inside to wait and eventually he just walked in the door. Curious, some of the group went outside and could find no footprints in the snow leading back to the boat or to the door. Qassim had shared with me that he had the ability to "travel" anywhere he chose. He mentioned that he had traveled in such a manner to the United States before, but he said it was difficult for him to see clearly there. He asked me if I knew why that would be. I said I didn't know. He then explained that it was because there wasn't much "spiritual light" there.

Sufi Master Najm Razi wrote in 1256:

If the Light rises in the Sky of the heart taking the form of one or more of several light-giving moons, the two eyes are closed to this world and to the other. If this light rises and the utterly pure inner man attains the brightness of the sun or of many suns, the mystic is no longer aware of this world nor of the other, he sees only his own Lord under the veil of the Spirit: then his heart is nothing but Light, his subtle body is Light, his material covering is Light, his hearing, his sight, his hand, his exterior, his interior are nothing but Light, his mouth and tongue also.

As we learn more about the holographic nature of the universe, our bodies need to be included in that holographic model. A 3-D hologram is pure light. If indeed the universe and our bodies are holograms, it's not too difficult to understand the phenomena of the light body scientifically, as discussed above. It is really just a question of acquiring a deeper sense of perception, one that sees beyond the apparent solidity of our world. David Bohm once commented, "The universe is frozen light."

We can access or re-enter this level of the original Clear Light perception through various means. It's interesting that in the Judeo-Christian mythos we have the notion of "fallen" mankind. Perhaps we could use the term *collapsed* equally. Our fallen state is actually a quantum collapse. Man is trying to undo the collapse through spiritual and religious means. However, one of the most readily available means is meditation. During the collapse into localized selfhood, the entire energy field also collapsed into a stepped-down mind state that now appears as dualistic consciousness, the mind that functions on the basis of thinking instead of knowing. It divides the unified field of Quantum Intelligence into imaginary parts, such as subjects and objects. This gives the individual the sense of being separate from all "others" and one's own deepest holistic self-nature. Through meditation methods and other more direct means, one is able to experience the original condition again.

The thinking mind is always fixated on stories related to the individual self. This reinforces the sense of separate selfhood by validating its existence as an independently existing entity. So we become locked in a dimension of our own creation through thought and imagination. By simply taking a position of observing the mind's phenomena instead of being the active promoter of its mental activities and stories, the personal identity shifts into an open state of consciousness that is not so tightly identified with its imagined role in the stories. This is similar to quantum phenomena reverting from a localized, fixed particle state into an undefined open wave state once again.

As discussed earlier, in meditation there is a specific state called *samadhi* or non-dual awareness. In samadhi there is no longer a fixed identity located in specific time and space. The essential nature of consciousness is pure Quantum Intelligence. All manifestations arise like reflections appear in a mirror in which Quantum Intelligence is the unchanging clear glass of the mirror and appearances are its reflections. We can sit in a comfortable manner and simply take the position of being the *observer*. At first, it may help by labeling thoughts as they arise by mentally noting "that's a thought." We begin to differentiate our pure observing from its activities. Notice how thoughts seem to appear on their own; notice how they disappear all on their own as well. Notice in the gap between two thoughts that your observing awareness is still present, even in the absence of thoughts. It's this observing awareness that is present during thought and during the absence of thought that we wish to highlight. This observing awareness has not been part of the mind's collapse. It is always unchanging and is therefore our royal road to the consciousness of original Quantum Intelligence. In relying on this method of pure observing, the collapse into dualistic states of self-centered consciousness is reversed. We eventually discover that this *pure observing* IS the awareness of original Quantum Intelligence present in *all* states of consciousness. It is not hidden or covered up. It is that which is reading these words written on this page. Look back at what's looking out your eyes and you will recognize that Quantum Intelligence to be your true nature that is looking.

Question: Are there examples of individuals who have managed to discover and activate their Quantum Intelligence or Quantum Mind?

Answer: I am sure there are many, but I don't think that the condition of Quantum Intelligence is continuous for most. This may be the case with inspired poets, artists, scientists, mystics, and inventors. But one group of individuals seem to offer a rather curious ability to see reality through the eyes of Quantum Intelligence more so than most other traditions. For more than sixteen hundred years, there has been a tradition in Zen in which a Zen master attempts to awaken a student through invoking the Quantum Intelligence of the student directly. One of the methods for this is the *koan*. A koan is a sort of mind puzzle that the student is supposed to wrestle with until an enlightening insight occurs. Some famous koans are: "What is the sound of one hand clapping?" or "Show me your face before your parents were born." The student works on these and presents various answers to the master over time. After exhausting all possible logical and rational explanations, the student in utter desperation may eventually break through into exposing and recognizing his own Quantum Intelligence. In this moment, the answer is totally obvious and he finally gains approval from the master for it. The answer could be expressed as a simple blink of his eye or a tapping on the table. Both answers making no sense to an outsider but perfect sense to the Zen master.

In the science of quantum computing, there exists a similar paradox. In a normal binary-based program, the information is processed as either a 0 (zero) or a 1. But quantum computation is based on 01; the 0 and the 1 are not separate choices of either/or, nor are they combined. They are both a 0 and a 1 at the same time. How can that be? That is a good koan, which only makes sense in quantum.

Also in the Tibetan traditions of the Great Perfection (Dzogchen) and Mahamudra, there are methods called "direct introduction" and "pointing out the true nature." In these traditions a master has a one-on-one exchange with a student and points directly to the Quantum Intelligence that is present and active but not recognized. Through a skillful "pointing out," the student may experience a sudden and authentic insight that erupts from within the Quantum Intelligence itself. This would be a flash of enlightened mind. The student is then directed to rest in that insight, allowing time for all sources of instability to arise and release until the original flash of insight becomes a permanent awareness.

Question: You discussed having an out-of-body experience when you were in Denmark. How does that experience relate to what you call Quantum Intelligence? Does that mean that our "personal" aspect of Quantum Intelligence has the ability to reincarnate?

Answer: As *localized* Quantum Intelligence, we are an aware continuum of experience. It could be said that we are a quantum mind, a dimensionless point of knowing awareness without boundaries or center. This is best represented by the image of a crystal sphere. This transparent and invisible crystal sphere is our quantum mind as it appears localized. It is surrounded by an energy field, the energy of its radiance. It is in this energy field or aura that memories regarding our continuum of experience are stored. It has the ability to perceive directly without the body's sensory systems. At death or during any out-of-body experience, this sphere of awareness leaves the body. It has the option to reincarnate or continue without a physical body. In the Tibetan traditions, it is taught that our clarity is seven times more intense and precise than it is within a physical body.

I have had several absolutely clear past-life memories that correlate completely with current life situations and tendencies. For example, I can recall vividly how I died just before inhabiting this lifetime's body. I was living in Europe and had just walked out of a café. Without observing properly, I walked into the street and was hit by a truck that came from the right. I felt myself float out of the body while seeing my body lying on the street with blood pouring profusely out of the right side of my head. As I started to float higher above the scene, I sensed this meant I was dying, and I desired not to abandon the body yet. I floated back into my head, at which point I felt an excruciating pain from the crushed right side of my skull. The pain was too intense, so I let go and floated up and away. From the earliest years in this life, I've always had horrible migraine-like headaches on the right side of my head so painful that I would curl up in a ball. I remember vividly being around five or six years old during one of these headaches. My mother took me to the doctor, but they could find no physical cause. Many years later, as a young adult, I had a past-life regression therapy session in which this memory came up. After recalling my violent death in detail, the headaches vanished and have never returned. I share this story in greater detail and several other memories from earlier lifetimes in my second book, *The Way of Light*. These memories had powerful and profound linkages to current life circumstances and proclivities. For me, there is no question that I have lived many times before.

Question: How can one develop this Quantum Intelligence for oneself?

Answer: Specifically, by studying the information presented in chapter 5. All three methods I present there should be sufficient. The appendix has detailed meditation exercises such as the "Opening the Eye of Wisdom" practice.

However, what I consider to be the essence of enlightenment, the real pith instruction that would hit the mark, is recognizing the "*knower or knowing quality*" within all experience. In every experience, whether as the mental phenomena of thoughts, images, and emotions, or as the phenomena of sensory perception with the five senses, there is always a *knowing* present. As we familiarize ourselves with this knowing quality, at first it will be defined as a "witness" to experience. This *knower* seems separate from what we experience. But if we look more closely, we notice it is not just a naked knowing but has some sense of identity, like "I am" knowing. If we then examine closely this sense of *I am*, we discover a complete story of personal identity that we see is made up wholly of individual thoughts as memories and mental images all strung together. If we then examine each of these thoughts and images, we discover that none of them has any enduring substance or solidity. We discover the empty aspect of all thoughts to be the same: empty, impermanent, without any inherent or independent existence. At some point we may realize that our sense of personal identity is therefore empty too, because it is nothing more than our empty thoughts about identity. There is no substance or solidity to any of it.

When the mind recognizes that the "*I am*" sense as a separate witnessing knower is purely imagination, a mere play of empty thoughts, then a moment of exquisite clarity may arise wherein the impersonal *naked knowing* of all experience reveals itself in conscious awareness. It is this naked knowingness without any sense of personal referencing that is our true enlightened nature. Its more like aware space rather than some kind of localized entity. Once recognized, we bring our awareness to rest in this naked knowing, free of personal self-definition, again and again until stable. A wisdom, a gnosis, arises with each fresh moment of recognition that reveals the core nature of being, the natural state of the aware knowing. This self-arising wisdom is the wisdom of enlightenment. To be enlightened is to recognize that the original *knowingness* as awareness is the Quantum Intelligence that has always been present since the beginning and has never been tarnished or subject to change.

Chapter Seven

Integration: The Merging of Wisdom, Love, and Life

> **The eye through which I see God is the same eye through which God sees me; my eye and God's eye are one eye, one seeing, one knowing, one love.**
> **—From the Sermons of Meister Eckhart**

We can only discuss *being* and *awareness* up to a point. That point is when our mind becomes oriented into resting as an attentive and alert presence that is *totally* relaxed. We have no topic in mind. We are just being and observing, not thinking about or judging our experience. Everything is allowed to be as-is, internally as thoughts, feelings, and perceptions, and externally as events and happenings. *Let be.* When we accrue some proficiency in this, a clear state of awareness spontaneously arises. As this clarity deepens, a sense of knowing who and what you are spiritually also arises. Leaving this as-is, the sense of being an observer dissolves, and there is a perfect non-dual integration of awareness and its field of perception. This is sensed as *oneness*. Again you just leave this condition of oneness as-is, and even it yields to a further condition of indescribable, vivid transparency, as though you are a clear window without a frame.

At some point the thinking mind enters again with an effort to grasp intellectually what has just occurred. At this moment of mental grasping, the dualistic state of subject and object reappears, and a sense of being a separate viewer arises. Through a subtle cognitive relaxing, the subjective sense of self dissolves revealing transparency once again. The five senses are open and alert but with no sense of someone seeing and hearing. There is just a naked seeing, hearing, feeling, and perceiving. The mind is completely still in clarity and presence, yet totally relaxed. One then continues in this natural equipoise without effort or will.

The Buddha was approached and asked by a person named Bahiya to reveal the insight necessary to realize enlightenment:

> "Teach me the Dhamma (supreme truth), O Blessed One! Teach me the Dhamma, O One-Well-Gone, that will be for my long-term welfare and bliss."

> The Buddha responded: "Then, Bahiya, you should train yourself thus: In reference to the seen, there will be only the seen. In reference to the heard, only the heard. In reference to the sensed, only the sensed. In reference to the cognized, only the cognized. That is how you should train yourself. When for you there will be only the seen in reference to the seen, only the heard in reference to the heard, only the sensed in reference to the sensed, only the cognized in reference to the cognized, then, Bahiya, there is no 'you' in terms of that. When there is no 'you' in terms of that, there is no 'you' there. When there is no 'you' there, you are neither here nor yonder nor between the two. This, just this, is the end of samsara (suffering)."

> Through hearing this brief explanation of the Dhamma (supreme truth) from the Blessed One, the mind of Bahiya right then was liberated. Having shared this teaching with Bahiya, the Blessed One left.

This is the teaching regarding simply to allow seeing, hearing, tasting, smelling, feeling and cognizing to occur without thoughts and stories intervening, including without the subtle thoughts of *I am* seeing, *I am* hearing or *I am* thinking. One is also not engaging thoughts with more thoughts, but just *noticing* a thought appearance like any sensory perception. There is no sense of "I am thinking" or "my thoughts". Thoughts just appear, owned by no one as they come and go. Just nakedly perceive without a center point of self-consciousness, as a newborn infant would experience its world.

If and when the mind arises with its grasping tendency again, as the central viewpoint of subjective experience as *I am*, you may feel separate from the total perceptual field. If you relax that grasping, the state integration will arise once again. This is the art of our practice. This subtle art continues until the mind no longer attempts to grasp the experience intellectually or worries about how to maintain the holistic integration and keep it from going away.

Imagine you are in a river, flowing with the stream in a most comfortable and playful frame of mind. Suddenly you are standing on the beach alone, shivering and wet. You wonder how this happened. You can't figure out how to simply jump back in the water. You are now a spectator on the sidelines. Our natural condition is oneness flowing in total integration *as* the river. Through the action of the mind's grasping energy, the subject-object dichotomy arises. In this instant consciousness assumes a specific vantage point. It becomes self-conscious and perceives the world of experience but as though separate from it. When we feel this separateness, which leads to a sense of fragmentation, suffering of some sort is sure to follow, and our spiritual quest, the return to oneness, begins.

I would like to refer to this moment of separation as the arising of self-consciousness. A subjective self-viewpoint arises in consciousness when it is no longer cognitively integrated with the total field of experience. Instead it is observing experience along with a fixed idea of a separate me and a separate world being self-consciously observed. What is interesting is that this process is not something that happened in our transcendental cosmic past. Rather this arising of *apparent* separation occurs constantly along with the dissolving into oneness.

Through our practice and insights, we may come to a clear intuitive knowingness of aware *being*. But now we can ask, "what is *being* doing"? Our life is not just living in a static state removed from movement and activity. We have bodies that are constantly doing things in the world. Where do the realms of *being* and *doing* meet? Is it possible to be fully integrated within our doingness? I would like to suggest that we experience this integrated state daily during our doing, and more often in our doing than in our moments of stillness. We think we have to sit in our meditation posture in perfect stillness to realize oneness or enlightenment. We miss the moments of perfect oneness that arise throughout our day because during those moments we are in oneness. When you are truly in it, oneness is not noticed. Otherwise you would be outside oneness looking at it.

A good analogy might be concentrating on an activity in which you are fully engaged in, whether it's a sport, an artistic endeavor, making love, or washing the dishes. You are one with the action, the *doingness*, when fully engaged. You completely forget yourself in the doing. This is authentic oneness. This is why many Zen masters have advocated physical labor or cleaning as a good Zen practice. You become totally one with your activity. This is the purpose of all the Zen aesthetic and martial arts, like brush paint-ing, tea ceremony, flower arrangement, kendo, Zen archery, and aikido, to mention the most well known of Zen arts. The practice is to come to a state devoid of all self-consciousness, which hap-pens to be the purpose of Zen meditation. So there is another way to discover this original state of oneness outside of sitting medi-tation practice. To discover oneness through an activity is even more powerful in life. Then *all* that you are doing is your practice.

In recent years, this pleasurable total absorption in our daily activities has been called "flow" or "being in the zone." It's not a deliberately focused mindfulness, as we may be too self-conscious in order to forget ourselves completely in the action.

> *To study Buddhism is to study the self. To study the self is to forget the self. To forget the self is to be enlightened by all things.*
> —*Dogen Zenji, thirteenth-century Japan.*

In his book *Zen in the Art of Archery*, Eugen Herrigel docu-ments his experiences training under a Zen master who was also a master of *kyudo*, the art of archery. Herrigel learned that one needs to remove the personal self and all intentional will from an action in order for the ultimate consummation of execution to occur. Once it occurs, the action seems to happen on its own. One discovers a "higher power" within yet beyond oneself. The higher power conducts the activity without interference from personal volition. The master referred to this higher power as It. He would say things like, "Let It conduct the activity." Ideally, a spontaneous action would arise of itself and the result would be quite perfect.

After several years of training, Herrigel had an opportunity to see the effectiveness of this self-less method of action. The mas-ter invited him to come to the archery range one night. Here is Eugen's recounting of that evening's events:

I seated myself opposite him on a cushion. He handed me tea, but did not speak a word. So we sat for a long while. There was no sound but the singing of the kettle on the hot coals. At last the Master rose and made me a sign to follow him. The practice hall was brightly lit. The Master told me to put a candle taper, long and thin as a knitting needle in the sand in front of the target, but not to switch on the light in the target sand. It was so dark that I could not even see its outlines, and if the tiny flame of the taper had not been there, I might perhaps have guessed the position of the target without any precision, though I could not have made it out.

The Master "danced" the ceremony. His first arrow shot out of dazzling brightness into deep night. I knew from the sound that it had hit the target. The second arrow was a hit, too.

When I switched on the light in the target-stand, I discovered to my amazement that the first arrow was lodged full in the middle of the black, while the second arrow had splintered the butt of the first and ploughed through the shaft before embedding itself beside it. I did not dare to pull the arrows out separately, but carried them back together with the target. The Master surveyed them critically. "The first shot," he then said, "was no great feat, you will think, because after all these years I am so familiar with my target-stand that I must know even in pitch darkness where the target is. That may be, and I won't try to pretend otherwise. But the second arrow which hit the first, what do you make of that? I know at any rate, that it is not 'I' who must be given credit for this shot. 'It' shot and 'It' made the hit. Let us bow to the goal as before the Buddha!"

Similarly, the apostle Paul said:

"It is no longer I who live, but Christ who lives in me."

We could just as easily say:

"It is no longer I who live, but *It* who lives in me, and *It* is the doer."

The point is that there is certainly a higher power at work that, if not personally interfered with, can accomplish great things effortlessly.

There is something formlessly created

Born before Heaven and Earth

So silent! So ethereal!

Independent and changeless

Circulating and ceaseless

It can be regarded as the mother of the world.

I do not know its name

Identifying It, I call It "Tao"

Forced to describe It, I call it Great...". (Lao Tzu)

If we can live our lives completely free of self-consciousness in all that we do, our life flows harmoniously and brings benefits of joy and satisfaction. Being free of self-consciousness is the same as absence of ego. The ego's energy transforms into the pure clarity of attentive action in total nowness. This does not mean that we need to be engaged in activities of a religious or spiritual nature or in a humanitarian endeavor. Any activity that brings a sense of pleasurable engagement in total absence of self-consciousness will do. It could be as mundane as washing your car, engaging in a sport, hiking in compelling scenery, or making love. Whatever it is, it requires that one be totally absorbed in the action, yet in a context free of pressure or duress. Once these moments are savored, it is possible to bring this attentive and naked presence unconsciously to all that we do. The key is to bring the activity to a point of total absence of self-consciousness. And it is not wise to "check out" if you "feel" the absence of self-consciousness during the action; that is tantamount to becoming self-conscious to see if you are free of self-consciousness.

Remember, when ego as self-consciousness transforms into the cognitive energy of the activity, no inner witness notices the quality of the performance. Most often, an indicator that a moment of absence of self-consciousness has occurred is a cognitive time distortion. People often ask after such experience, "Wow, where did the time go?" It was a timeless moment because without the ego as self-consciousness, there is no time.

People have moments outside of time in total oneness and absence of self without having studied, meditated, or thought about such topics previously! Becoming cognitively alert to these moments of oneness, you begin to notice the subtle and delicate quality of the flow, like the flow of the Tao. You live in the flow as being the flow, in whatever you do.

As you learn to live in the natural flow of life, absent of self-consciousness, the orientation begins to shift from *awareness* to becoming grounded in your own heart of compassion and intimate caring. From the brilliant clarity of sight and sensory experience centered in the head, your center of consciousness descends into the depths of the heart, where you find peace, contentment, love, and joy. These qualities of the heart aren't the result of attainments or virtuous actions, rather they are intrinsic to your very Being. By simply inviting your consciousness into the heart, you come to know your most intimate nature. You discover your reason to live, your purpose for being. There is divine wisdom, peace, and stillness in the heart that only awaits your conscious arrival. Many traditions have spoken of this wisdom and of the heart as the seat of divinity in man.

Not many years ago, I had a lucid dream that symbolized the path of the spiritual heart and our light of awareness. I would like to share that dream.

> I found myself flying high above the beautiful Na Pali cliffs of Kauai, Hawaii, in the warm clear skies above deep, azure blue waters reflecting ripples of sunlight that glistened and gleamed as I glanced below. I noticed I was completely naked and was floating on the heated thermals of air that sustained me, with only my outstretched arms as wings. It was a moment of total joy and freedom, unlike any I had ever previously known. The rich emerald green lushness that blanketed the volcanic cliffs that extended more than a thousand feet to the shores below was suffused with life's vibrancy and its urge to survive and grow. I took this all in as a lover gasps in pleasurable joy, inhaling the intoxicating panorama as never wanting the moment to fade away, attempting to hold it within forever. And in that same moment, the thought arose, "How can I be flying high in the air without wings or some means of support?" With that thought, I began to fall, turning and whirling slightly as I descended to the waters below. I sensed I needed to face upward and land with arms and legs spread outward,

as I would crash and splash on the waters below. I had an easeful sense of letting all fear of death go and to just release and relax, trusting in the perfection of everything telling me so.

Having fallen several thousand feet, my body finally merged with the sea. There was no pain or break in consciousness as everything was clearly felt and seen. I gently sank beneath the waves, descending into the depths as I looked upward at the bright light of the sun, which shone on the surface as seen from below. As I was drawn deeper into the depths, the sun's warm glow began to fade, brightness fading slowly to darkness and darkness fading to black, utter blackness like crystalline black glass. All sense of self dissolved, but never the overarching sense of being. Yet in this darkness I was embraced and comforted by a sense of total love and acceptance. There existed a stillness and peace that I couldn't imagine ever leaving. With that thought, I caught a glimmer of light from above. The total darkness was penetrated by the light that seemed to work in tandem with the darkness below. It drew me upward from the depths into its radiance and warmth. My world became luminescent and filled with a gentle light that pervaded the waters all around me. The light seemed so vibrant with life. It was inviting me into its exquisite realm of sheer vividness and causeless delight. The feeling of being totally aware and conscious eclipsed the receding darkness as the day does the night.

It was in this moment that I awoke in bed. My eyes suddenly opened, looking up at the ceiling, laying on my back just as I had been in my dream. Something had changed, my perspective had shifted from feeling like I was looking out my eyes from within my head to experiencing that my conscious awareness was centered in my heart, and I was looking from my heart out through my eyes. There was the same feeling of inexpressible peace and contentment that I had known when in the deepest, most still place of the darkness. I didn't want to get up and leave the bed, the sense of peaceful contentment was just so captivating. But I did get up and got ready for my day. This sense of being centered in my heart in a state of deep peace and happiness lasted for several days. Later I found myself more seeming to be positioned behind my eyes. But I could always relax and allow my consciousness to descend again into my heart to experience the peace and contentment that always awaits my conscious surrender.

This dream symbolizes all the elements of my quest for the most profound wisdom, the understanding of my own inner nature, and the changeless qualities of Being. From flying high in the sensory realms of infinite beauty and sheer delight to the depths of the unknowing and the darkest night, I know it's all pervaded from top to bottom by our own ever-shining love and perfect light.

In many awareness or non-duality teachings today, the spiritual heart or its role in the process of liberation is not clearly understood. In most of the mystical traditions, the spiritual heart is given great emphasis. I thought it might be useful to explore this important topic a bit more in detail.

From one of the most famous proponents of the Advaita Vedanta tradition of India, Ramana Maharshi, comes many references to the idea that the Supreme Self or God resides mystically in the heart. This is not actually the physical heart, but often is described as an energy center or chakra associated with the location of the heart as the center of our being. Ramana Maharshi is surely not alone in his conviction.

What is called the heart is no other than Brahman (God)...

Call it by any name, God, Self, the Heart or the Seat of Consciousness, it is all the same. The point to be grasped is this, that HEART means the very Core of one's being, the Centre, without which there is nothing whatever. (Ramana Maharshi)

The Luminous Brahman (God) dwells in the cave of the heart and is known to move there. It is the great support of all; for in It is centered everything that moves, breathes, and blinks. (Mundaka Upanishad, Second Mundaka 2:1)

The Self is hidden in the lotus of the heart. Those who see themselves in all creatures go day by day into the world of Brahman hidden in the heart. Established in peace, they rise above body-consciousness to the supreme light of the Self. Immortal, free from fear, this Self is Brahman, called the True. Beyond the mortal and the immortal, he binds both worlds together. Those who know this live day after day in heaven in this very life. (From the Chandogya Upanishad, 8:1.1 2 4.3. Translated by Eknath Easwaran in *The Upanishads* (Petaluma, California: Nilgiri Press, 1987).

This heart within us is God Himself. (The Brihadaranyaka Upanishad)

The wise, who by means of the highest meditation on the Self knows the Ancient One, difficult to perceive, seated in the innermost recess, hidden in the cave of the heart, dwelling in the depth of inner being, he who knows that One as God, is liberated from the fetters of joy and sorrow. (Katha Upanishad, Verse 12)

The Sufis of Islamic mysticism also maintain that God is to be found in the center of the heart. The Eastern Orthodox Christian teachings known as Hesychasm also maintains that we find God by bringing our conscious awareness, or *nous*, positioned in the head, down into the heart. In Orthodox Jewish Kabbalah, the ultimate nature of God, known as *Ain Sof*, also resides in the spiritual heart.

Rumi the thirteenth-century Sufi mystic wrote:

> Only from the heart can you touch the sky.

> As you live Deeper in the Heart, the Mirror gets clearer and cleaner.

> I searched for God among the Christians and on the Cross and therein I found Him not. I went into the ancient temples of idolatry; no trace of Him was there... Finally, I looked into my own heart and there I saw Him; He was nowhere else.

From the Eastern Orthodox Christian tradition:

> You've got to get out of your head and into your heart. Right now your thoughts are in your head, and God seems to be outside you. Your prayer and all your spiritual exercises also remain exterior. As long as you are in your head, you will never master your thoughts, which continue to whirl around your head like snow in a winter's storm or like mosquitoes in the summer's heat. If you descend into your heart, you will have no more difficulty. Your mind will empty out and your thoughts will dissipate. Thoughts are always in your mind chasing one another about, and you will never manage to get them under control. But if you enter into your heart and

can remain there, then every time your thoughts invade, you will only have to descend into your heart and your thoughts will vanish into thin air. This will be your safe haven. Don't be lazy. Descend. You will find life in your heart. There you must live.

Attention to that which transpires in the heart and proceeds from it—this is the chief activity of the proper Christian life. (Quotes from the nineteenth-century Russian Orthodox monk St. Theophan the Recluse)

Tibetan Dzogchen and the native Bon religion of Tibet, both teach that the ultimate ground of being resides in the heart. In these traditions, the heart itself is known as the *Mother Light*. Our conscious awareness in the head is known as the *Child Light*. It is taught that originally the Child Light arose from the Mother Light, and complete enlightenment occurs when the Child Light merges again into the Mother Light in the heart. The two have never actually been separate, but the mind creates the appearance of separation. When we die physically, the Child Light, our consciousness, sees the bright and shining Mother Light through a crystal channel connecting the head with the heart. It appears as though we are looking down a tunnel of light into the heart.

This tunnel in Tibetan is called the *kati*, the crystal channel of light. The Child Light, as our consciousness, sees the bright white Mother Light, the radiance of our own intrinsic warmth, as unconditional love at the end of the crystal channel in the heart center. The child then moves toward and merges into its mother, or self-origin, at the heart. This is complete and permanent enlightenment. However, this can also be accomplished while still alive, but is more rare than common. We would notice that person to be "all heart."

All practices in the Tibetan tradition of Dzogchen aim at this result. Our sense of separation is just this mentally conceived divide between the Child and Mother Light, the Clear Light of our Absolute Nature. The prodigal son or daughter finally returns home.

When our consciousness fully enters the heart, we notice a completely different experience of being. The sense of separation is absent, as all duality between an independent localized self-awareness and our Absolute Beingness is resolved. There is profound peace, settled-ness, and contentment.

> When the mind eventually sinks into the Heart, undisturbed bliss is overwhelmingly felt. There is then a feeling which is not divorced from pure awareness, as an example, head and heart become one and the same. (Ramana Maharshi, GR, 80)

In this moment we feel our essential nature to be unconditional love, a pure radiance of Being's self-luster. We don't have to do anything to earn this; it's always been present eternally. Through our engagement with our mind's activities and distractions, we haven't bothered to notice our true nature. As Jesus taught, "The kingdom of God is within you" (Luke 17:21).

In 1978 I was in Kathmandu, Nepal, and had the rare privilege of being accepted into a Tibetan Buddhist lineage at Swayambhu Temple by the master known as Sachyu Tulku. This lineage was called the Karma Kagyu and dates from the time of their greatest master Milarepa, who lived in Tibet approximately one thousand years ago. Sachyu Tulku was eighty-four years old at the time and died a few months later. At first he performed the necessary initiation rituals called empowerments, and then his main instructor taught me the initial energy and visualization practices.

Weeks later, when I returned to the United States, I sat down one evening in my room with the intention of doing the main practice as I was taught. It was very simple as far as these types of practices are concerned. I was to visualize a golden Buddha in the center of my heart. He was radiant and glowing with golden light. From his heart center, rays of light emanated outward in all directions, bringing the energies of love and compassion to all sentient beings in the universe. In order to accomplish this visualization practice, I first had to generate the sense that at the center of the Buddha's heart resided an infinite power of love and compassion. That power could relieve the suffering of all beings in the universe. With that clearly in mind, I visualized the outward streaming of this powerful light reaching all ends of the universe. As I remained with this visualization for several minutes, suddenly it felt as though the center of my heart broke open and an experience of total love flowed through my being. I have never known such a deep feeling of pure love and compassion before or since. This profoundly spiritual experience drove me deeply into the innermost core of my existence where I discovered the heart light of my true nature, a guide that would never fail to lead me in the right direction.

Here is a very simple meditation that can offer a means for everyone to enter their own inner sanctuary of the heart. First, find a quiet space or room for the practice. Find a comfortable seat: sitting on a chair or on a cushion on the floor. Align your posture so that your spine is straight. Close your eyes and just notice your breathing for several minutes. As you breathe in, imagine the energy of your breath going into the center of your heart chakra in the center of your chest. Breathe gently like this while focusing on your heart chakra. When your mental energy has settled down and you feel relaxed and open, remember a time when you felt strong love for someone. Once you have even the slightest feeling of love in your heart, remain focused on that feeling. Let that feeling grow and attract your attention more and more. As you become proficient with this practice, your attention and consciousness drift deeper into the space of the heart. It will seem that your consciousness has descended from being centered in your head to being located in your heart. In this new condition you discover a deep peace, contentment, and loving joy. You may also notice the sensation that the heart is like an aperture on a camera that is now opening or dilating ever wider. This is a good indication that your practice is moving in the right direction. Continue with the exercise as outlined above, and the rest develops spontaneously and organically. If you like, you may also engage in the practice I was taught in Nepal and described above. But above all, forget your thoughts and imagined stories, and relax completely in this clear and aware heart space of your true nature.

After being on this quest for forty-six years, I have noticed that Western culture values the intellect more than the heart, of course not in all cases, but it seems generally true. However, you can realize that the heart has its own wisdom and only fully comes to life when the dualistic thinking mind is transformed into Clear Light. The main job of the intellect is to assure strategic survival of the organism. The main job of the heart's wisdom is to bring us home to our essential goodness, perfection, and joy. We are beings of Light, and through recognizing our own awareness to be the Clear Light of the Heart, we find we are already home.

When our existing consciousness transforms into its essential wisdom nature, which is its sustaining basis, we see the world as sacred and divinely perfect just as it is. Our mandala of experience does not become a realm of blank emptiness. Rather it is seen as it has always been: a rich seamless web of relationships and luminous energies that delight the eye and inspire spontaneous joyful creativity. In this realm of infinite freedom, we discover that the woof and warp of those relationships are grounded in compassion and love, the mandala's pulse and lifeblood. We can enter this mandala through the wisdom path or through the path of unconditional love. The completion of either is the completion of both.

Inspire yourself along this journey by opening your heart to love all beings and life. Delight yourself in nature's splendor and dance freely in the Clear Light of your own self-recognition from moment to moment.

Here is a short story from the Tibetan Dzogchen tradition. Keep in mind that *Dzogchen* means the "Great Perfection" in English. The term points to the inherent perfection of our true nature and of all reality. We won't find this Great Perfection restricted to being some extraordinary spiritual experience alone. Rather, we discover the immediate intimacy of the Great Perfection in every moment of experience. Every moment, every mental event, every feeling, every perception is an appearance and expression of the perfect Buddha Nature however it appears.

> Nyoshul Lungtok, who later became one of the greatest Dzogchen masters of recent times, followed his teacher Patrul Rinpoche for about eighteen years. During all that time, they were almost inseparable. Nyoshul studied and practiced extremely diligently, he was ready to recognize the enlightened awareness, but had not yet had the final *introduction to that state* by a master of the Great Perfection. Then, one famous evening, Patrul Rinpoche gave him the introduction to that state. It happened when they were staying together in one of the hermitages high up in the mountains above Dzogchen Monastery in Tibet. It was a very beautiful night. The dark sky was clear and the stars shone brilliantly. The sound of their solitude was heightened by the distant barking of a dog from the monastery below.

> Patrul Rinpoche was lying stretched out on the ground. He called Nyoshul over to him, saying: "Did you say you do not know the essential nature

of awareness?" Nyoshul guessed from his tone that this was a special moment and nodded expectantly.

"There's nothing to it, really," Patrul said casually.

"My son, come and lie down over here: be like your old father." Nyoshul stretched out by his side.

Then Patrul Rinpoche asked him, "Do you see the stars up there in the sky?"

Nyoshul answered, "Yes."

"Do you hear the dogs barking in Dzogchen Monastery?"

Nyoshul again answered, "Yes."

"Do you hear what I'm saying to you?"

And again Nyoshul responded, "Yes."

"Well, the meditation of the Great Perfection is *this*: simply *this*."

Appendix: Summary of Methods and Exercises

Essential Basics of Practice

The most primary practice is the non-practice of just being awareness, your default condition. This would be practiced in a formal meditation session, sitting with no agenda, yet fully present without mental or conceptual engagement. This practice is actually the fruit of practice, yet it appears as our current condition in each moment. There is no sense of self or conceptualized objects in this non-dual state of presence. When as this naked awareness, one just continues as this vivid and alert awareness in all the twenty-four hours of the day and night in total relaxation. On successful development, the chakras are fully open and the subtle energies flow in the central channel. The body feels transparent to your inner perception, and the mind is utterly clear with blissful feelings circulating within your inner channels.

If your condition is not as described above, it is advisable to practice calming meditation for at least a half-hour daily, just sitting with your spine straight, eyes focused on a point either on the wall or on the floor, with no moving of the eyes, no mental agenda, and just observing your breathing. If thoughts, emotions, or sensations arise, just notice them but do not judge or engage them. They dissolve on their own. You can break this up into two sitting sessions per day if necessary.

Here is another practice that can be quite helpful when you're in an uncomfortable or unclear state of mind:

The Self-Liberation of All Conditions

Notice your current state of mind. What is in your mind in this moment, exactly as it is? Whether it is a story, thoughts, self, or an emotional state, just observe the condition. See if you can find any solidity to it, anything that is stable and permanent. After looking at the condition in this way, notice that it is an empty appearance that your attention sustains and energizes. Notice the empty, transparent aspect of the condition.

Next, notice the awareness that is present in that noticing. Observe the quality of that aware noticing. Is there anything solid about it? Color? Shape? Is it just an aware emptiness? Having resolved that the noticing empty awareness is completely transparent, now notice the original condition again. Has it vanished? Has it lessened? Has it been transformed into empty awareness? If not, repeat the steps above until the condition "self-liberates." It will anyway because all appearances and conditions are impermanent, empty, and unborn.

Exploring the Blueprint of the Subtle Body

You could imagine the central channel to be approximately as wide as your thumb, pale blue on the outside and pinkish red on the inside. The general appearance is one of semi-transparency, as though glowing from within. The side channel of the right side is luminous red and the left channel is luminous white. For females the channel colors are reversed. They are both approximately as wide as your little finger. This is good information to know, but we won't be doing any specific practices with the side channels per se. By focusing on the chakras and central channel alone, the side channels respond automatically. When you are able to direct your prana or inner energy into the central channel, the side channels become inactive. Likewise, when your mind is engaged in dualistic thought along with negative emotional energies, the side channels are active and the central channel is closed and inactive. Again, the goal of the energy practice is to bring the prana into the central channel to open and activate your chakras fully. To the degree that you succeed in this effort, you experience states of consciousness that are otherwise inaccessible to most human experience. Our ultimate goal is to bring the energy into the central channel upward from the base of the spine into the crown chakra. You can experience complete enlightenment from this method alone.

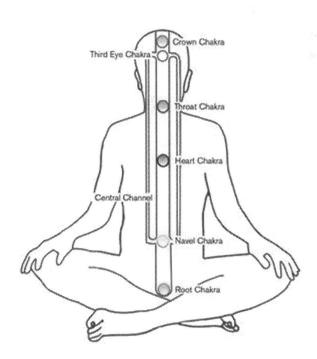

The Main Subtle Body Practice Sequence

For some, the energy practices may be too intense because they tend to release contracted energies and reveal buried emotional blockages. This can be uncomfortable and disorienting. The practices I have shared here should be done gently with no effort to force the inner energies. You *should not* exert yourself through intense breathing exercises or breath retention while engaging in these exercises. Go slowly and learn to feel your limits gently. But you do not know how you will do until you experiment with your own energy a bit. If you start to feel uncomfortable, cease the practice. Take a walk in nature, do some physical exercise, or engage in some pleasant activity. It is certainly enough to stay with the basic *clear awareness resting practices*, like sky gazing and the calming meditations.

First, sit in an upright position. You can do this while sitting a bit forward on a chair so as to get the spine as straight as possible. I prefer sitting on a cushion on the floor yoga style. How you arrange your legs is not so important; just be in a stable position. Rest your hands comfortably on your legs as you like. Your spine must be straight.

Close your eyes and notice your breathing. Feel the breath as it passes in out and out of your nose, and feel how your lungs expand and relax with each breath.

Next, sense the central channel running from the bottom of your spine to the fontanel. You don't have to visualize it clearly, just sense that there is an energy channel running within the spinal column from bottom to top. Focus on the topmost point of your head, which is slightly behind the center of the skull. You can locate the fontanel with your finger. It may feel like a small indentation or soft spot on the skull. Imagine there is an energy center there that vibrates subtly just below the surface of the skull at the fontanel, perhaps an inch or two below, within the brain.

At some point your attention settles on this correct location naturally, so don't worry about getting it just right. Focus on the general area. Once you sense some sort of energy movement that holds your attention, you have located the crown chakra. Focus on that energy point for at least five minutes or so. Remember, you don't have to visualize or imagine anything; just focus your attention on the general location. The crown chakra is present in all people; you just have to notice it. It should feel like a slight vibration or energy pulsing. Keep that as your point of reference. Try to keep your attention on that point as often as possible throughout the day and evening, especially when about to fall asleep. Try to do twenty minutes of sitting meditation every day with only this practice. Once you have success in locating the crown chakra, your meditation should bring about a relaxed and calm state of consciousness. At times you feel like you could remain focused on the crown chakra for hours because it's so pleasant. By all means, continue as long as it's comfortable. A key aspect of practice is to release all tension and to find oneself in a state of total relaxation of body and mind. By relaxing completely while remaining vividly alert, the inner channels and chakras open fully allowing a very pleasant sensation to pervade the entire body. Your state of mind will be expansive and serene. By engaging in the practice, the entire inner subtle energy body becomes toned and activated.

When you are competent with this practice routine, you may use this expanded version that I use:

1. I focus on the base of my spine.

2. I try to sense a warm energy or tingling sensation at the base of the spine or slightly higher.

3. I relax my breathing, making deep and slow breaths.

4. I relax completely without thought, with my eyes closed.

5. As I breathe in slowly, I draw the sensation from the bottom of my spine upward.

6. As I breathe out, I mentally hold the inner energy where it is, then breathing in, I continue to bring it upward.

7. Sometimes it enters the heart chakra on the way and produces a sense of joyousness.

8. I keep it at the heart for as long as it lingers there.

9. When ready, I continue bringing it upward with each in-breath, not letting it go lower.

10. As the blissful sensations develop after several minutes, I bring the energy to the top of my crown at the fontanel.

11. A strong sense of spaciousness grows along with bliss sensations.

12. I hold my breath gently and look straight up with my eyes closed, focusing my eyes upward as though to see the top of my head from inside. I fixate on that and focus on an imagined point of light at the crown, yet within the skull.

13. A sensation begins to grow that pulsates at the third- eye and base of the spine.

14. I stay with that for as long as I can.

15. I relax and just witness.

16. With my eyes closed, I look out forward into space through the third-eye chakra. I integrate my awareness into that vast spatial depth.

Recognize your awareness that is experiencing what's occurring. Notice that you are the empty, aware context in which all phenomena occur as content. Rest as that recognition, with no agenda.

If you feel an uncomfortable pressure in your head, visualize an opening at the fontanel and your prana flowing upward into the space above your head. That should relieve the discomfort.

If at anytime you are uncomfortable while doing any of these practices, take a break and go for a walk or engage in some activity to take your mind off the practice. Always use your intelligence and never push yourself in any way. Relaxation and gentleness are always key.

Sky Gazing

When your mind is relatively calm and clear, then you should practice *sky gazing* or *space gazing*, in which you focus on the sky without moving your eyes, or space gazing, in which you gaze into the space of a room but not at any physical object.

Bring your sense of awareness to the eyes and sense that it is merged with the outer space of the sky or the empty space of the room between your eyes and the wall. Rest like this free of all deliberate thinking for ten minutes, and eventually extend the session as long as it's comfortable. Keep your eyes free of all movement, but blinking is fine. Breathe slowly and quietly through the mouth, with the mouth just slightly open. The longer you practice, the more your mind and awareness become transparent and clear. Notice the resulting empty, clear awareness to be your essential nature. You are not the body, your mind, or your thoughts. You actually do not need any other practice besides this one. It incorporates many benefits that would accrue from engaging in many other practices.

Inner Light Practice

Close your eyes and notice the light from an exterior light source on the inside of your translucent eyelids. Notice where the light is and where your sense of awareness is centered. Perceive sounds and notice how the sounds appear to be inseparable from your awareness. Rest in that sense of inseparability for as long as comfortable. Notice your empty awareness from time to time.

Notice the light at your eyes on the inside of your closed eyelids again. Sense that the light fills your skull, which seems empty, without brains, just filled with light and awareness. Rest in that spacious condition for as long as is comfortable.

Slowly open your eyes, but only slightly. Notice the space of the room without focusing on any objects. Observe how your awareness seems inseparable from that space of the room, and rest in that spacious awareness. Then notice how your skull seems transparent, with no limitation to your awareness, and rest in that transparency of awareness.

Close your eyes again, and from inside your skull, imagine looking upward to the crown of your head. Notice if there is any pulsing or vibration at the crown. If so just rest in that moment of sensation for several minutes.

Next notice if there is any pulsing or vibrating sensation at the tail bone or in the area at the bottom of the spine, and if so, again rest in that sensation for several minutes.

Next notice the crown point again for several minutes. Now notice the point at the third-eye to see if there is any pulsing or vibrating, and if so, rest in that condition for several minutes.

Alternate between noticing the crown point, the third eye, and the tailbone for several minutes again and again until sensations appear at all three points and remain stable, as this brings the subtle energies into the central channel.

Then notice the light at the eyes again. Notice the clear empty spaciousness within your hollow skull and its transparency. Rest in this clarity for several minutes.

Open your eyes slightly and rest in that clear awareness for as long as comfortable. Without any agenda, be clear and present without intentional thinking.

End your session, but do not engage again in deliberate thinking or conceptualizing. To do so collapses the quality of open spaciousness. Practice like this as often as possible.

Zen Tradition Practice

In Zen Buddhism, the main practice is to sit in the correct posture without focusing the mind on any topic, other than perhaps noticing your breathing. Correct posture means sitting with the spine and neck straight and the chin pulled in a bit. Whether sitting on a cushion on the floor or on a chair, keeping the back straight is very important. It allows the inner energies to flow up the central energy channel naturally. You are usually instructed to focus attention within the navel chakra, a point about two inches below the navel. By doing this consistently with alert concentration, the energy in the navel chakra increases to the point of overflowing downward toward the base of the spine, where it enters the central channel. From the downward pressure on the energy entering the central channel, the prana begins moving up the central channel to the crown chakra. When the energy enters the crown chakra, true non-dual samadhi or meditation, occurs. Ordinary ego-consciousness, which is centered in the brain and crown chakra, transforms into pure awareness. This heralds the point of total realization. Your sense of ego dissolves automatically, like ice melting into water. At this time you feel your inseparability and oneness with the universe and experience profound insights into the nature of reality. In the early Buddhist teachings, there are groups of texts called the Prajnaparamita Sutras that state that all material forms are essentially empty of any inherent, independent existence, but yet this emptiness expresses itself exactly as the forms we perceive, like holograms. This becomes direct experience and is fully realized.

Opening the Eye of Wisdom

> The eye through which I see God is the same eye through which God sees me; my eye and God's eye are one eye, one seeing, one knowing, one love. (From *The Sermons of Meister Eckhart*)

I learned this practice from Qassim, my Sufi teacher in Kashmir. When done properly, a powerful state of intuitive awareness arises and perhaps complete enlightenment.

Sit quietly on a chair or a cushion on the floor for a few minutes with the eyes closed. Let all thoughts and desires come to stillness. Notice that all thoughts are empty, meaning they have no substance or permanent basis, like empty clouds. Notice that all your stories about everything are also empty. Next notice how your sense of personal self is also just another story based on memories and is, therefore, also empty, like a dream. Notice that the space of your inner awareness is also empty and is the context in which thoughts and stories arise, along with your sense of self. Recognize that you are this changeless empty awareness.

Imagine there is a large single eyeball embedded in the center of your forehead looking outward. It is above the location of the third-eye chakra. It's quite large and tapers backward on both sides contacting the ears. Once comfortable with that visualization, get the feeling that you don't have to "imagine" the eye, but rather it has always been there unnoticed. Just rest as though you are looking into the room through that eye, with your two eyes closed. Remain in this contemplation for at least fifteen minutes at a time and repeat as often as possible. When you notice thoughts, remind yourself that thoughts are empty, stories are empty, and your sense of personal self is empty. Again notice that the space of your inner awareness is also empty and is the context in which all thoughts, stories and sense of self arise. Recognize that you are this changeless empty awareness.

It is also excellent practice to do this exercise lying on your back when going to sleep. Fall asleep while doing this practice yet maintaining a sense of vivid clarity in the area of your forehead.

The results may appear gradually or suddenly. An extremely clear state of transparency that is full of wisdom and insight arises in the area of your forehead. When fully opened, you realize the nature of reality and your true nature. That's why this eye is called the wisdom eye. Clairvoyance and other extrasensory perceptions may also arise. The wisdom eye is recognized in Kabbalah, Sufism, Tibetan Buddhism, Kundalini Yoga, and Shamanism.

For further information regarding retreats or practice questions, contact Jackson Peterson at ejackpete@yahoo.com or through his website: www.wayoflight.net

You can also join Jackson's Facebook group, Transparent Being, where he answers questions and offers advice: www.facebook.com/groups/436183323088781/.

10562046R00125

Printed in Great Britain
by Amazon